"Most of us probably think we know a lot about Jesus. After all, we've read all the Red Letters in the gospels. But you never really know or fully understand Jesus, His stories and ways, until you know the world in which He lived. A big thanks to my friend Bill Marty who has lifted the lid to give us a peek into the culture that shaped the message and methods of Christ. This book is a great opportunity to get to know Jesus better!"

—Dr. Joseph M. Stowell
President, Cornerstone University,
Grand Rapids, Michigan

"Life in our high-tech, fast-paced society places modern readers of the Bible at an extreme disadvantage when they seek to understand the biblical backdrop behind the story. Dr. Bill Marty solves that! His careful but plain explanation of The World of Jesus is a gift to everyone who desires a rich grasp of Scripture. Keep this close when you study the Bible and you will not be disappointed."

—J. Paul Nyquist, PhD
President, Moody Bible Institute

THE WORLD OF JESUS

Books by Dr. William H. Marty

The WORLD OF JESUS

Making Sense of the People and Places of Jesus' Day

DR. WILLIAM H. MARTY

BETHANY HOUSE PUBLISHERS

a division of Baker Publishing Group
Minneapolis, Minnesota

Published by Bethany House Publishers
11400 Hampshire Avenue South
Bloomington, Minnesota 55438
www.bethanyhouse.com

Bethany House Publishers is a division of
Baker Publishing Group, Grand Rapids, Michigan

Printed in the United States of America

Library of Congress Cataloging-in-Publication Data
Marty, William Henry.
    The world of Jesus : making sense of the people and places of Jesus' day /
Dr. William H. Marty.
        pages cm
    Summary: "Bible professor teaches readers about the world Jesus lived in
and the time between the Old and New Testaments"—Provided by publisher.
    ISBN 978-0-7642-1083-9 (pbk. : alk. paper)
    1. Palestine—History—To 70 A.D. 2. Jews—History—586 B.C.–70 A.D.
3. Judaism—History—To 70 A.D. 4. Jews History—168 B.C.–70 A.D. 5. Jesus
Christ—Historicity. 6. Bible. O.T.—History of contemporary events. 7. Bible.
N.T.—History of contemporary events. 8. Church history—Primitive and early
church, ca. 30–600. I. Title.
DS122.M37 2013
220.95—dc23   2013002244

The internet addresses, email addresses, and phone numbers in this book are accurate at the time of publication. They are provided as a resource. Baker Publishing Group does not endorse them or vouch for their content or permanence.

Cover design by Gearbox

13 14 15 16 17 18 19   7 6 5 4 3 2 1

To my devoted wife, Linda, who loves me
because of and despite who I am.

And to my daughter, Talitha,
loving wife of Jeff, and one of the most
compassionate persons I know.

And to my son, Stephen,
husband of Monica and father of my two
grandchildren, Judah and Isaac.

When I was younger, I was blessed
by my wife and my children,
and now that I'm older, I am also blessed
by my two grandchildren.

God is indeed good!

Contents

Introduction

The Time Has Come

This is a book I've wanted to write for several years. I have been teaching Old Testament and New Testament Survey for more than three decades, and as part of the latter, I teach about the history of Israel between the Testaments. In most Bibles, you simply turn a page from Malachi, last book in the Old Testament, to Matthew, first book in the New. But in fact, there was an intertestamental period between the Old Testament and the New—four centuries of history, happenings, changes and developments, kingdoms and empires, births and lives and deaths. Knowing what happened during that era is crucial to understanding the earthly life of Jesus Christ and the New Testament settings and events.

My lectures and books on the subject are detailed and technical. Often I've thought about how useful it would be to make this material accessible, available to everyone. That's what I've sought to do in this book—provide reader-friendly information and insight on the world of Jesus.

Why Is This Important?

When reading through the Bible, turning from the Old Testament to the New is like visiting another country. A few years ago, I had the opportunity to teach in Russia for about a year. It was an incredible experience. The people were wonderful, not like I had anticipated because of the relatively recent hostilities between the former Soviet Union and the United States.

It was also challenging. To prepare, I studied Russian history and culture. I even took a course in the language. Though I would have an interpreter, I knew I should know enough Russian to ask where to find food, water, and the bathroom. My preparations helped, yet still I was surprised by the differences between the two nations. While many Russians looked like Americans, I quickly realized their language and culture were completely different from mine. Anyone who has visited another part of the world can appreciate this.

The world of Jesus was not the Old Testament Hebrew world. Like the United States now, Israel was multicultural, including a combination of Aramaic, Greek, and Roman influences. The people looked Jewish but spoke Aramaic and Greek. The Bible that many used was a Greek translation of the Old Testament (see chapter 2). Some dressed like Jews; others dressed and lived like Greeks. When Jesus began his ministry, his chief opponents (Pharisees and Sadducees) were from groups the Old Testament doesn't even mention.

In addition to worship in the temple, Jews met in synagogues for prayer and for reading the Scriptures. Jesus and Paul taught in synagogues. Jesus was executed by crucifixion, a Roman method of punishment. Paul was sent to Rome for a hearing before the emperor. And most of all, the Jews were not a free independent nation. Their land was occupied by the Romans and ruled by client kings who weren't descendants of David. It wasn't even a single nation; the land had been divided into provinces. Foreign soldiers were everywhere. The Jews paid taxes to Rome. One of Jesus' disciples was a tax collector.

To understand these elements, and many more, we need to find out what happened there in those centuries between the Old and New Testaments.

What's the Plan?

I have tried to write the story of Israel-between-the-Testaments in plain English. In addition to the Bible and my lecture notes, for additional information on this period I have used 1 and 2 Maccabees, books about the Jewish war for independence, and Flavius Josephus, a Jewish historian.

I have divided the pertinent years into four distinct periods:

Persian (539–331 BC)
Greek (331–143 BC)
Jewish—Maccabean/Hasmonean (143–63 BC)
Roman—Life of Christ/Early Church (63 BC–AD 70)

Regarding the Persian period, in the first chapter I have briefly interwoven some happenings from the Babylonian era, which you might find familiar from the Old Testament, in order to explain and illustrate how Israel went from being a powerful kingdom to a people overpowered and in exile. Regarding the Roman age, as you'll see in the book's later chapters, I have extended beyond the era between the Testaments so as to include background information for the Gospels and Acts. I have set off some blocked material in a contrasting font to provide more in-depth information on certain key individuals and events, and timelines open most chapters to help clarify the historical sequence. There are discussion questions after each chapter, and you'll find a glossary of terms at the end of the book.

The era between the Testaments is often called "the Four Hundred Silent Years" because during that time God stopped speaking to his people through the prophets. From the time of Malachi, the last Old Testament prophet, God was "silent" until the coming of John the Baptist. Mark's gospel summarizes John's message: "After me will come one more powerful than I, the thongs of whose sandals I am not worthy to stoop down and untie. I baptize you with water, but he [the Messiah] will baptize you with the Holy Spirit" (Mark 1:7 NIV1984).

Even though God was not then speaking through prophets, he had by no means forgotten his promise to send a Savior. He was actively working through history to prepare the world for the coming of his Son. In his first announcement of the "gospel," Jesus declared, "The time has come. . . . The kingdom of God is near. Repent and believe the good news!" (Mark 1:15 NIV1984).

Israel's Actions, God's Promises: A Look Back

To find out why Israel was in exile near the end of the Old Testament timeline, we need to look back into the nation's history.

About four thousand years before, Abraham had lived in the city of Ur in Mesopotamia (northwest of the Persian Gulf). God appeared to him and promised to bless him, make him into a great nation, and bless all the earth through him. God's promises to Abraham were passed to his son Isaac and then to Isaac's son Jacob, or *Israel*, as he was later known. Israel's twelve sons became the heads of Israel's twelve tribes.

Out of jealousy, his brothers sold Jacob's favorite son, Joseph, to slave traders who took him to Egypt. God blessed Joseph there, and ultimately he became an influential ruler, the nation's second-in-command under the Pharaoh. Because of a famine, Jacob's sons had to go to Egypt just to buy food. When they saw Joseph was alive, they thought he might kill them. But he invited them to move their families there and promised to provide for them.

Over approximately four hundred years, the children of Israel (Jacob) multiplied and prospered in Egypt. In fact, the *Hebrews* (as they'd become known) became so numerous that the Egyptians feared they might take over. The king (the new Pharaoh) enslaved them, and he ordered the midwives to kill at birth all their male children. Moses was born into this desperate, lethal situation. When he was grown, God called him to deliver his people from slavery. Their exit out of Egypt marks the beginning of national Israel.

Instead of leading the Israelites directly to the Promised Land (Canaan), which God had promised through Abraham, Moses led them south to Mount Sinai. While they were en-camped, God gave Moses a set of legal codes. The Law of Moses became the new nation's constitution.

Because the Israelites refused to trust God, they spent the next forty years trekking around in the desert. When they arrived on the plains of Moab (east of modern-day Israel), Moses told them God would bless them in Canaan if they were devoted to him, yet he warned that if they abandoned him to serve other gods he would expel them from the land and scatter them over the earth.

God also promised that they would return to him and that he would restore them to their Promised Land. The Law's promises and warnings were similar to a customary section in ancient treaties known as "blessings and curses," in which a suzerain pledged to bless his servants yet warned of severe consequences for breaking the covenant. The blessings and curses became Israel's guiding principle through the rest of the Old Testament story. When they honored God, he blessed the nation. When they disobeyed him, he judged them. Eventually their disobedience would result in exile from the land.

After the death of Moses, Joshua led the children of Israel's conquest of Canaan. They were now a complete nation and a people devoted to the Lord. They had a constitution, the Law of Moses, and they had land, a place to call home. Joshua and his generation loved the Lord and served him.

However, the next generation was disobedient and suffered the consequences of breaking the covenant: God allowed their enemies to enslave them. When they were oppressed, the people cried out to God; he answered their prayers by raising temporary leaders (judges) who defeated their oppressors. This cycle in which they persisted—the cycle of disobedience, oppression, and deliverance—continued for approximately three hundred years.

Because Israel did not have a king like other nations, the people asked and then insisted that the prophet Samuel give them one; Samuel anointed Saul as Israel's first king. David was the second, and Solomon, David's son, the third. During the 120 years of the "united monarchy," when the king and people were faithful to worship and serve the Lord, he protected them. They enjoyed peace and prosperity when they obeyed; when they disobeyed, God used other nations to judge them.

After Solomon died, the united monarchy came to a sudden end; the single kingdom divided into two nations. Ten tribes broke away and formed the kingdom of Israel in the north, and the tribes of Judah and Benjamin became the kingdom of Judah in the south.

The northern kingdom was a disaster from start to finish. The frightening statement *"He did evil in the eyes of the Lord"* was true of *all* its nineteen kings. Though warned by the prophets, kings and people were incurably infected with idolatry and spiritual apostasy. Because they abandoned God, he brought on them "the curses" of covenant violation. In 722 BC, the mighty Assyrians invaded and scattered Israel's population all over their empire.

Judah, the southern kingdom, endured about two hundred years longer. This was in part because some kings listened to the prophets' warnings. Still, of the nineteen kings and one queen, only eight did "what was right in the eyes of the Lord." The others copied the sins of the kings of Israel, and they too teetered on disaster's precipice for ignoring their covenant obligations.

Finally the Babylonians, who had conquered the Assyrians, invaded Judah, captured Jerusalem, and took thousands of captives as prisoners to Babylon in 586 BC. The Bible states that the exile was not the result of superior military strength but because the people of Judah had broken their covenant with the Lord and refused to obey the prophets.

Despite both Israel's and Judah's unfaithfulness, God was faithful to his covenant promises. As he had pledged through Moses: "When you are scattered among the nations, if you will return to me with all your heart, I will have mercy on you and bring you back to the land."

The Babylonian exile lasted seventy years.

The World of Jesus begins with the return from the exile. I hope you enjoy the story.

Note: If you would like more information on Israel, see *The Whole Bible Story* (Bethany House, 2011).

1

Homeward Bound

The Persian Period

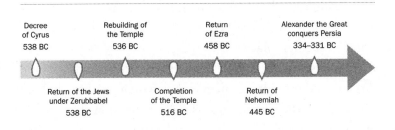

Decree of Cyrus 538 BC	Rebuilding of the Temple 536 BC	Return of Ezra 458 BC	Alexander the Great conquers Persia 334–331 BC
Return of the Jews under Zerubbabel 538 BC	Completion of the Temple 516 BC	Return of Nehemiah 445 BC	

Introduction

(The Jews had been in exile for approximately seventy years. The Persians had conquered the Babylonians; Cyrus, king of Persia, issued a decree that opened the door for the exiled Jews to return to Judea.)

The messenger had sprinted from the palace all the way to the house of Zerubbabel, a Jew who worked for the Persian government. "Zerubbabel! The king has given his word— granted permission to go back! We can go *home*."

As soon as Cyrus announced his decision, Daniel the prophet, an advisor to Persia's king, had sent his most trusted servant with the unbelievable news. Under his "return to normalcy" dictum regarding conquered nations, Cyrus had reversed the policy of the Babylonians.

The year was 539 BC when the God of Abraham, Isaac, and Jacob moved the heart of Cyrus to proclaim that the Jews could return to Jerusalem and rebuild the temple of the Lord (Ezra 1:2–4). The prophet Jeremiah had foretold it truly; the exile had lasted about seventy years (Jeremiah 25:11–12).

The Fall of Judah

Before looking at the return to Judah, we need to backtrack momentarily and note how the Jews ended up away from there in the first place.

When Israel first entered Canaan, God promised he would protect and provide for them if they worshiped him and not the gods of the Canaanites. Israel remained faithful for almost two centuries, but after David and Solomon were gone, they began to worship other gods. The prophets warned the kings and the people that God would judge them for spiritual apostasy. They didn't listen. In 722 BC the Assyrians conquered Israel in the north and dispersed thousands of the chosen people throughout their territories. That empire fell when the Babylonians captured Nineveh, the capital of Assyria, in 612 BC.

Under Nebuchadnezzar's leadership, the Babylonians invaded Judah three times. First, in 605 BC, they took Daniel and other young men from the royal family as hostages to Babylon but allowed Jehoiakim to remain as king. When his son, Jehoiachin, rebelled, Babylon re-invaded (597 BC); they took captive the king and thousands of others, and they sacked the temple and took all the treasures Solomon had

Cyrus

More than a century before the Babylonians conquered Judah and dragged the Jews into captivity (c. late seventh century BC), Isaiah prophesied, *by name,* the people's restoration through the as-yet-unborn "Cyrus" (Isaiah 44:28–45:7). He identified Persia's future king—a non-believing, foreign ruler—as God's "shepherd" and "anointed one," a divinely commissioned deliverer.

Cyrus originally ruled Anshan, a small kingdom within the empire of Media. In 550 BC he rebelled against Media and captured Ecbatana, its capital city. Unlike other ancient rulers, Cyrus was a benevolent conqueror and did not slaughter captives or plunder cities. His "return to normalcy" principles honored local deities and allowed captured people to return to their land. This was wise, too—by showing respect he gained his subjects' support.

After consolidating control of the Persian Empire, Cyrus began expanding his kingdom to the west and then to the east. He conquered the kingdom of Lydia, captured the Greek cities of Asia Minor (modern Turkey), and then marched east to attack Babylon. But instead of bracing for a lengthy siege, its priests and people welcomed him as "king of Babylon" and "ruler of the world."

When Cyrus took over the Babylonian realm, the seventy years of exile were nearly over (Jeremiah 25:11–13; 29:10). Daniel realized the time was almost complete and sought the Lord in prayer, fasting, sackcloth, and ashes (Daniel 9:1–19). God was faithful to his covenant promises, in 539 BC motivating the "Edict of Cyrus" (Ezra 1:1–4) that willing Jews could return to their land. On top of permission to go home, Cyrus supplied the returnees with gold and silver and returned the treasures the Babylonians had taken when they plundered the temple (Ezra 6:1–5). Approximately fifty thousand Jews returned to rebuild their nation and God's house.

Cyrus placed his son Cambyses in charge of the campaign to conquer Egypt while he led a small force to put down a rebellion in the east. Mortally wounded in a minor battle, he was buried in Pasargadae, his capital.

Widely held to be one of the world's greatest conquerors, to the Jews, Cyrus was the Lord's "anointed one," chosen to fulfill God's covenant promises to his people.

placed in it. Nebuchadnezzar placed Zedekiah on the throne but marched against Jerusalem a third time (586 BC) when he also rebelled. The Babylonians overran towns and cities, captured Jerusalem, burned the temple, and demolished the city walls. They executed Zedekiah's sons, then blinded Zedekiah and took him to Babylon in bronze shackles.

Nebuchadnezzar, thinking to reestablish some security and stability in the area, appointed a Jewish governor. Gedaliah strove to restore communities, encouraging those who'd hidden in the hills or fled to other nearby lands during the invasion to return and settle and replant the vineyards and fields. But Ishmael, the leader of a band of Jewish diehards, assassinated Gedaliah and killed many of the Jews who'd joined him; they also slew many of the Babylonians whom Nebuchadnezzar had left for their protection. Then Ishmael and his followers, taking captives from among the survivors, fled and sought refuge with the Ammonites.

The remaining Jews were terrified of Nebuchadnezzar's wrath, given not only that once again he would see the region as troublesome but also that Jews had murdered his men and his governor of choice. Johanan and a group of officers pursued and tried to capture Ishmael; he escaped, though Johanan was able to rescue the hostages. Fearing Babylonian reprisals, Johanan and others fled to Egypt even though the prophet Jeremiah warned them that the flight was a fatal mistake. Sure enough, when the Babylonians attacked Egypt, Jews who had sought safety there were killed or captured.

When Zerubbabel heard that the exiles could return, all those decades later, his heart overflowed with joy. Still, many memories also flooded his mind. God's people had lost so very much. Thousands upon thousands had grown old and died, or had been born and raised, with another life, in another land. Judah, no longer independent, was an empire's province.

The Exile

The exile, though in itself not excessively harsh, was a national disaster. The deported Jews weren't treated as prisoners of war; however, they faced losing their treasured unique religious and ethnic identity. Providentially, what helped them to persevere was the preaching of the prophets, who said that while the exile was divine judgment, it wasn't the end of the nation. God had not permanently abandoned his people.

The prophets inspired the exiles with promises of a glorious future, one that, meanwhile, would include several developments.

A New Empire

Nebuchadnezzar, the last of the powerful Babylonian rulers, had invaded Judah three times. In 605 BC he took Daniel and other selected Jewish youths as hostages and demanded that Judah pay tribute. When King Jehoiakim of Judah stopped sending it, Nebuchadnezzar invaded again (597 BC) and took captive Jehoiakim with thousands of others, including the prophet Ezekiel. Zedekiah was allowed to rule as king until he too mutinied; this third time (586 BC), the Babylonians devastated the land, destroyed Jerusalem, looted the temple, and hauled off untold thousands into exile. After subsequent events, the survivors abandoned Jerusalem and Judah ceased to exist as a nation.

In Babylon, Daniel and his friends were trained to become counselors to Nebuchadnezzar. God was with them; they excelled in their training, and the prophet Daniel began his remarkable career as an advisor to kings. His ministry spanned over eight decades.

After ruling for forty-three years, Nebuchadnezzar died (561 BC). Three other kings ruled briefly before the empire fell during the rule of Belshazzar.

Even with Babylon under siege, Belshazzar had not been concerned—he believed the great fortress could not be breached. He and a thousand nobles were partying as the city fell to the Persians.

After excessive drinking, Belshazzar ordered his servants to bring the gold cups looted from the temple in Jerusalem. Up to that point, the Babylonians had not defiled the temple's treasure.

God acted decisively. Mysteriously, a human hand appeared and, in their view, began writing on a wall. Belshazzar, now terrified, offered to make the man who could interpret the writing the third-highest ruler in his kingdom.

No one could. The king sent for Daniel.

Daniel, after telling him to keep his gifts, proclaimed the writing to be a verdict, for his arrogance and his disrespect for the "Most High God": The words *Mene, Mene, Tekel, Parsin* mean "numbered, numbered, weighed, and divided." Belshazzar's days were numbered; he had been weighed, and he did not measure up to God's standards of righteousness even for a pagan ruler.

Unlike Daniel, Belshazzar did not live long. That same night a combined force of Medes and Persians entered the city and killed him. Darius, the Mede, took over the kingdom, at the age of sixty-two. (There is uncertainty regarding the identity of this Darius. He may have been appointed by King Cyrus to rule over a portion of the vast empire, for to what "the Medes and Persians" had controlled was now added all the Babylonian holdings.)

The Persian conquest was according to God's sovereign plan for his people. As we have seen, Cyrus issued his decree in 538 BC, ending the exile and freeing the Jews to return to Judea.

A New Place of Worship

If the Jews in exile were to continue observing the Law of Moses, they needed a place to worship. Clearly they wouldn't have been able to go to the temple even if the Babylonians hadn't destroyed it. The solution was the synagogue. (Based on passages like 1 Samuel 15:22–23 and Psalm 51:14–17, they substituted the study of the Torah [Scriptures] and prayer for sacrifices.)

Ezekiel the prophet, taken captive in the second invasion, was also a priest. He started a ministry in his own house in Tel-abib. God's people had based their beliefs and patterned their lifestyles on the Scriptures; to preserve their heritage as "people of the book," Ezekiel invited a group of elders to study together. Though this isn't certain, the exiles apparently organized the synagogue on the model of studying the Scriptures in his home.

Any community with ten Jewish males could organize a synagogue. Each synagogue had a "head elder" and was governed by a council of elders.

The synagogue functioned as a religious, educational, and cultural center. Jews would meet there on the Sabbath and other holy days for prayer and reading of the Torah, after which a qualified individual would explain the passage.

The Synagogue in the New Testament

Both Jesus and Paul ministered in the synagogue.

Jesus was born in Bethlehem, six miles from Jerusalem, but lived in Nazareth—to the north, in Galilee—until he began his public ministry at about age thirty. He had worshiped and attended school in its synagogue. After being tempted by Satan in the Judean wilderness (see Matthew 4), he returned to Galilee and began teaching in their synagogues.

The usual order of service included recitation of the Shema (see Deuteronomy 6:4), prayer, a prescribed reading from the Law or the Prophets, a reading of Scripture in Aramaic, a message, and a closing benediction. Visitors, if qualified, could read and give the message. Jesus, in Nazareth (Luke 4:14ff.), was asked to do so and chose Isaiah 61:1–2, about Israel's Messiah.

Isaiah had foretold that Messiah would be anointed by God's Spirit and would preach good news to the poor, freedom to captives, and recovery of sight to the blind. Jesus abruptly stopped in mid-verse, with "to proclaim the year of the Lord's favor" (and then sat down), because that—God's gracious offer of salvation—was the part of Isaiah's prophecy he came to fulfill at his first coming. He did not read the second half of verse 2: "and the day of vengeance of our God," because that is about judgment on the world when he returns.

It was customary to stand while reading and then to sit while explaining the passage. With all eyes fixed on him, he said, "Today this Scripture is fulfilled in your hearing."

All were amazed, and some were willing to recognize him as their long-awaited deliverer, but the majority, knowing him only as "Joseph's son," thought he was preposterous in claiming *he* was the one the Scriptures promised.

Jesus held his ground, charging them with stubbornness just like their ancestors who'd rejected God's prophets. Enraged, they hauled him out of Nazareth and tried to throw him over a cliff. But he "walked right through the crowd and went on his way" (Luke 4:30).

On their first missionary journey, Paul and Barnabas would go to the island of Cyprus and then to what now is western Turkey. In the synagogue at Antioch in Pisidia, after the reading, the elders invited them to speak, and Paul seized the opportunity. After reviewing Israel's history, he proclaimed Jesus to be the fulfillment of all God's promises to Israel. The response was similar to what met Jesus in Nazareth: Some were convinced and wanted Paul to speak again on the following Sabbath.

The following week the synagogue was packed, and many believed. However, the majority rejected Paul's claims about Jesus. Accusing him of insulting them, they organized opposition. Evading the threat to their lives, Paul and Barnabas went to Iconium. That synagogue's reaction to Paul's preaching was the same: A large number of Jews and Greeks believed, and others started a "smear campaign." The missionaries moved on after learning of a plot to stone them (Acts 13:14–14:7).

Children learned to read by studying the Scriptures. Jews also met there to make friends and to socialize with one another.

A New Language

One development of the exile was an additional language for the Jewish people. The Babylonians and Persians spoke Aramaic, and out of necessity the Jews learned it. Some even became more conversant in Aramaic than Hebrew, and over time it became the common people's primary language (though the religious leaders prioritized Hebrew). The transition was not difficult because of the similarity between the two tongues. Many Jews at the time of Christ spoke three languages—Hebrew, Greek, and Aramaic.

As soon as Jesus crossed the Sea of Galilee and stepped out of the boat, Jairus, a synagogue ruler, fell at his feet, begging him to heal his terminally ill daughter. Before they reached his house, a messenger said she'd died. When Jesus arrived, he said, "The child isn't dead; she's only asleep" (Mark 5:39 NLT). The mourners laughed, but he put them outside, took the girl by the hand, and said, "*Talitha koum!*" Aramaic for "Little girl, get up" (v. 41).

When Jesus prayed, he sometimes addressed God as *Abba,* a unique and highly personal Aramaic term for "Father." His cry from the cross in Aramaic, "*Eloi, Eloi, lama sabachthani*" means "My God, my God, why have you forsaken me?" (Matthew 27:46).

A New Name, a New Occupation

In his early ministry in Jerusalem, when Jesus cleared the currency exchangers and other vendors from the temple, the

Jews protested, "What's your authority for doing this?" (see John 2:18). In the New Testament, and most clearly in the gospel of John, Jesus' opponents are called *Jews*. However, until the Babylonian exile, the descendants of Israel had been called *Israelites*. Why were they all called "Jews" thereafter?

Apparently it was difficult to pronounce "Judahites" in Aramaic, so the Babylonians shortened the term.

Further, before the exile, the Jewish people were mostly farmers who lived off the land. When taken to Babylon, while they lost their land, they were not imprisoned or interned in camps. They were allowed to establish communities and, over the years, became merchants and businessmen. Some were sufficiently successful to become wealthy.

The Return From Exile

The challenge was daunting, to say the least. How would Zerubbabel move tens of thousands of Jews over a thousand miles? He put his assistant in charge of the government office where he served and quickly left for the home of Jeshua, the high priest. Jeshua had heard about the edict, and the two men agreed this was the hand of God. Though they'd been unfaithful, the Lord remained faithful to his people. They remembered his words through Moses:

> When . . . you are living in exile among the nations, if you will return to God and obey him with all your heart, then I will have mercy on you and return you to the promised land. Even if you are scattered all over the earth, I will gather you and return you to the land I promised to your ancestors. I will prosper you in the land. (Deuteronomy 30:1–4, author's paraphrase of NLT)

Many Jews had decided to stay in Babylon rather than face the hardships of traveling, resettling, and rebuilding. Those who *would* go had to organize: register the people by tribes, identify the priests and Levites, gather supplies, and collect furnishings for the temple. The Lord moved the heart even of those who did not go back to Judea to give generously for the journey and for the temple's rebuilding. Daniel, chief advisor to Cyrus, not only had influenced the issuing of the decree but also had convinced the king to return to the Jews all the gold and silver articles Nebuchadnezzar had taken from the temple. Ancient rulers were not known for compassion and generosity, yet God had not forgotten his people. Amazingly, as he had promised, he was restoring his people to the land by moving the heart of a pagan ruler.

Approximately a year after the pronouncement of Cyrus, Zerubbabel and Jeshua led the first group of exiles home. Scripture gives no details of this journey to Jerusalem, but undoubtedly it was both difficult and dangerous.

Esther

The book of Esther tells of how God providentially protected the Jews who decided to remain in Persia when they were threatened by a plan to eliminate them. During the reign of King Ahasuerus (Greek: *Xerxes*), who ruled from 486–465 BC, a young and beautiful Hebrew girl was chosen as queen to replace Vashti, who had been removed from her royal position for refusing the king's command to appear before him and his drunken officials at a banquet.

Several years later, Esther's cousin Mordecai discovered a plot to assassinate Ahasuerus. He told his niece; she informed the king, and the assassins were hanged. The event was recorded in the historical records, although Mordecai was not rewarded for what he had done.

Some time later the king made one of his officials, Haman, his chief of staff. An arrogant man, Haman expected everyone to bow to him. Mordecai refused.

Haman was infuriated. When he found out Mordecai was a Jew, he began scheming to kill all the Jews; he had his diviners cast lots (*purim*) to determine the opportune month to launch his ethnic cleansing campaign. And he needed royal sanction, so he convinced Ahasuerus that the Jews were a threat. When he also offered the king a huge sum of money for permission to exterminate them, Ahasuerus agreed and gave Haman his signet ring, a symbol of royal authority. Haman used it to endorse a decree addressed to the leaders of every one of the 127 provinces, authorizing the annihilation of every Jew in the empire on the thirteenth day of Adar, the twelfth month.

When Mordecai learned of the edict, he asked Esther for help. When at first she was reluctant to get involved, for by no means did she have unlimited access to the king, Mordecai persuaded her. Not only was she likewise in danger, he said, but also they should consider that God, providentially, might have placed her where she was in order to protect his people. She agreed.

Esther planned a dinner party for three. Then she donned her royal robes and made a daring surprise appearance before the king so that he might be reminded of her beauty and position. Ahasuerus, delighted with his queen, eagerly accepted her invitation to dine with his chief of staff.

For his part, Haman couldn't believe his astounding fortune. He *alone* was sought to spend a whole evening with the king and queen!

Ahasuerus so enjoyed the event that he offered to give Esther anything she wanted, even half of his kingdom.

The queen's response was unusual: She asked only that Ahasuerus and Haman come to dinner again the following night.

Haman's splendid evening turned sour when he was on his way home. He saw Mordecai, and he remembered how much he hated the Jew. Suddenly he couldn't think of anything else.

Back in his own house, in the midst of his complaints, his wife and his friends made a suggestion: He was a man of power; why didn't he make arrangements to have Mordecai impaled? (Impalement on a sharp pole was the preferred Persian method of execution.)

That night, at the palace, there was more providential intervention. The king couldn't sleep and ordered his servants to read to him the kingdom's historical records. When he heard the report of how Mordecai had foiled the assassination plot, he also found out Mordecai had never been rewarded.

The next morning Haman went before the king intending to seek permission to hang Mordecai. But the king had his own agenda and something entirely different in mind. Ahasuerus asked Haman what he would do, if *he* were king, for a man he wanted to honor.

Naturally, Haman thought the king was looking for a way to honor him, so he said he would dress the man in royal robes. He would have a crown placed upon his head. And he would parade him on horseback throughout the city, in the sight of all the people.

The king liked the idea. So he commanded Haman to honor Mordecai exactly as he had suggested.

Haman was devastated. But he was obligated to parade Mordecai all over Susa.

Later that day he returned home utterly humiliated. When he told his wife and friends what had happened, they told him he'd gravely erred in seeking to destroy the Jews. They may have known that others, like the Egyptians, had tried to destroy the Jews but instead had been destroyed by their God.

That same night, at the second party, the queen sprung her trap. In the middle of dinner, she asked a favor of the king.

"Of course," he said.

Esther then told Ahasuerus that there was a plan to exterminate her people, and she asked his permission for them to defend themselves.

The king was stunned. Esther, on Mordecai's stern warning, had concealed her ethnic heritage from the start; he had never known she was a Jew. Now he demanded the identity of "the man who has dared to do such a thing."

Esther answered, "An adversary and enemy! This vile Haman!"

The king was so furious that he stormed out to collect himself and determine exactly how he would proceed.

Haman, in abject terror, began pleading for his life. Just before the king returned, he collapsed next to Esther on her couch as he begged for mercy.

The king exclaimed, "Will he even molest the queen while she is with me in the house?"

As soon as the word left the king's mouth, they covered Haman's face. Then Harbona, one of the eunuchs attending the king, said, "A pole reaching to a height of fifty cubits [about seventy-five feet] stands by Haman's house. He had it set up for Mordecai, who spoke up to help the king."

The king said, "Impale him on it." So they impaled Haman on the pole he had set up for Mordecai. (Esther 7:8-10)

By law Ahasuerus could not rescind his former decree, so he issued another, again sent to all the empire's provinces, granting the Jews power to assemble and defend themselves against anyone who attacked them and then to plunder the property of anyone who did.

On the day after they defended themselves and, instead of being wiped off the earth, killed thousands, the Jews celebrated and memorialized their victory with the Feast of Purim, named after *purim,* the lots cast to determine the day for the attacks meant to eliminate them.

Though there are no specific references to Esther in the New Testament, the book is powerful evidence of God's protection of his people; by his hand their fate was reversed, and instead of being annihilated, they destroyed their foes. (On the cross, Jesus promised the repentant thief that on that very day he would be with Jesus in *paradise* [Luke 23:43], which is a Persian word meaning "garden.")

The story also emphasizes God's ultimate plan to save his people and destroy all their enemies. Though the Jews did not accept Jesus as Messiah at his first coming, God will preserve his covenant people until Christ returns, when "all Israel," or many Jews, will recognize Jesus as their Lord and Savior.

Rebuilding the Temple, and Further Returns

The people of Judah, once a mighty nation, now were a small remnant surrounded by formidable enemies. They needed divine help.

Jeshua and Zerubbabel had already decided what would be done first. Once the returnees had settled in their towns, they gathered in Jerusalem, built an altar, and began daily sacrifices, morning and evening. Jeshua explained that these were for rededicating themselves to God and obeying his Law.

In the second year (538 BC), they began the sacred task of rebuilding the temple. When they laid the foundation, the priests sang songs of thanksgiving, and the people gave a great shout of praise. The singing was so loud that even those who did not live in Jerusalem, including their enemies, heard the celebration.

Jews and Samaritans

Not everyone was excited about the return of the Jews. During the exile, Samaritans and other ethnic peoples occupied Judea. The Jews—from their perspective now illegal immigrants—threatened the Samaritans' possession of the land.

Still, the Samaritans at first offered to join the rebuilding, and Zerubbabel and the other leaders rejected their overture. Some of those occupying the land included Jews from the former kingdom of Israel (the northern kingdom). So why did Zerubbabel refuse their help?

The answer is that most of the Israelites had been scattered throughout the Assyrian Empire after Assyria overran Israel and captured Samaria in 722 BC. Half a century later,

King Esarhaddon (r. 681–669 BC) was continuing the Assyrian policy of deportation and resettlement and had brought people from various parts of his empire into the area that was formerly Israel.

The Israelites who hadn't been deported, those who stayed there all along, had continued to worship the Lord, but they also began worshiping the gods of other nations. Zerubbabel knew that God had sent his people into exile because of idolatry, and he recognized the danger. He was not about to open doors for the Judean returnees to interweave with those who served false gods, even if they did worship the Lord too. Plus, if the Samaritans were involved in rebuilding the temple, they could claim the right to worship there as well. Zerubbabel used a legal reason for refusing their help. He said, "We must build this house for the Lord, our God, as Cyrus has decreed."

Without Jewish cooperation, the Samaritans resorted to intimidation and threats. They also bribed government officials to stop the work, which was abandoned for about fifteen years. Then God raised up the prophets Haggai and Zechariah to encourage the returnees to complete what they'd started.

The Persian governor Tattenai tried to stop the work again, but the Jews persisted and appealed to King Darius I (r. 550–486 BC) for an official hearing. Tattenai sent a letter to Darius asking for a search of the archives to find out if Cyrus actually had given the Jews permission to rebuild the temple. Darius found the decree, and he ordered Tattenai to stop all opposition.

Darius also issued two other decrees. The first instructed Tattenai to provide funds for reconstruction. The second warned of severe punishment for anyone who interfered with the Jews—he was to be impaled on a beam from his own house, and his house was to be made into a garbage heap.

In the decades that followed, the Jews and Samaritans became bitter enemies. The Jews would complete the Jerusalem temple, and eventually the Samaritans would build their own temple at Mount Gerizim (near the biblical Shechem, in Samaritan territory).

Ezra the Priest

The return of Zerubbabel was the first of three "returns" from exile. In 458 BC, Ezra and a small group of priests, Levites, and temple servants made the six-hundred-mile journey back to Judea. Ezra, a priest, was devoted to the spiritual renewal of the returnees through the study, application, and teaching of the Law (Ezra 7:10). He brought with him articles the Babylonians had looted from the temple and letters from King Artaxerxes I (r. 465–424 BC) authorizing him to restore services in the temple.

When he arrived in Jerusalem, Ezra offered sacrifices to the Lord and delivered the king's letters to the governors of the region. It wasn't long before the Jewish leaders reported to him a shocking development. Some of the people, even priests and Levites, had married foreign wives.

The Law didn't prohibit marriage to foreigners. Joseph, for example, had married an Egyptian, Moses a Midianite. The issue was spiritual, not racial. By marrying foreigners who served false gods, the Jews set themselves up for abandoning the Lord, as with Solomon and his foreign wives (1 Kings 11:4). For the former exiles, the spiritual peril was so great that Ezra ordered drastic action: Those who'd intermarried were to put away their wives and children.

This issue reveals a primary threat to God's people because of the exile. He'd chosen the nation Israel to bring a blessing to all nations (Genesis 12:1–3), and ultimately he would fulfill his promise through Jesus, a descendant of Abraham and David (Matthew 1:1) but a Savior for the world (28:18–20). It was crucial that Israel protect its distinct ethnic identity. If Israel were assimilated into the nations, the messianic line and hope would be lost.

The rebuilding of the temple was essential for the preservation of Israel's faith through the centuries that followed. Though Zerubbabel's temple was disappointing in size and splendor compared to Solomon's, it nevertheless symbolized God's presence among his people.

In 20 BC Herod the Great began a massive reconstruction of it, a project so extensive the temple was renamed Herod's Temple. Christ's coming eliminated the need for a physical temple. Instead of residing there, God dwelt in Jesus and later in the church (John 1:14; 1 Corinthians 3:13).

Ezra being identified as a "scribe" (Ezra 7:6) most likely means he was a student and teacher of the Law of Moses, and according to Jewish tradition he was the first scribe. Over the centuries, the scribes became the Law's official interpreters, and they made judgments on religious and legal issues. By the time of Christ, their legal decisions had become official in oral tradition.

Many of the conflicts between Jesus and the religious leaders were about these scribal traditions. The Pharisees and scribes repeatedly accused him of breaking the Law. However, he never violated the Law of Moses. He often disregarded scribal interpretation of the Law because it violated the divine intent of the actual Law God gave to Moses for the people (see Matthew 23).

Nehemiah the Cupbearer

Even as a Jew in exile, Nehemiah held an important position. He was cupbearer to the king of Persia.

In 445 BC, Nehemiah's brother Hanani came from Jerusalem to Persia with distressing news. The situation back home was terrible. Jerusalem's gates and walls had been burned down, leaving the returnees defenseless. When he heard the report, Nehemiah wept and mourned, and then he decided to help.

Because Artaxerxes had previously issued a decree stopping the work on rebuilding the city, Nehemiah knew it would be hard for him to get permission to return. Before approaching the king, he turned to the Lord in prayer, confessing his sins and the sins of the people and asking God to assist him.

About four months later, Nehemiah went before King Artaxerxes. He told him about the situation in Jerusalem and of his prayer to the God of heaven. He asked the king for permission to return to Jerusalem to organize the rebuilding of the city and its walls. He also asked for letters from the king to the region's governors granting him safe passage and instructing them to supply the timber for the reconstruction. Artaxerxes granted both requests.

When the local officials heard that someone had come from Persia to help the Jews rebuild Jerusalem, they were extremely angry.

But Nehemiah wasted no time. Three days after arriving he made a secret night inspection of the walls. After assessing the situation, Nehemiah informed the Jewish officials, priests, and people of his purpose and plan for the walls.

When their enemies heard about his plan, they ridiculed the Jews and charged them with sedition. Nehemiah ignored their complaints and replied, "The God of heaven will grant us success."

Rebuilding the walls was not easy. In addition to their arduous labor, the builders had to stay alert for subterfuge and surprise attacks. But Nehemiah was a superb leader. He organized the workers into teams. While some toiled, others stood guard, armed and ready; they even took weapons with them when they bathed. When the workers became discouraged, Nehemiah assured them that God would help them.

In addition to the tasks and trials of rebuilding the city, Nehemiah had to deal with economic and social inequities. Some had been forced to mortgage their farms in order to pay the taxes imposed by Persian governors. Further, crops had been devastated by a famine; creditors were threatening to confiscate property. Nehemiah set the example of generosity and compassion. He loaned money, interest free, to those who needed help and challenged creditors to stop charging interest and repay interest they'd already collected. He said that this was the right thing to do before God and that God would hold them accountable for any exploitation of their Jewish brothers. The lenders followed his advice, and the financial crisis was resolved.

Work on the walls continued, and the project was completed in fifty-two *days*. This achievement was so remarkable that even foes admitted that the work had been done "with the help of God."

After the walls were finished, Ezra read from the Law of Moses to remind the Jews that they were a covenant people who had promised they would honor the Lord and faithfully serve him. Since most of the people spoke Aramaic, the language of the Babylonians, Ezra's assistants translated the Hebrew Scriptures into Aramaic, explaining the Law's meaning and application.

Nehemiah did have to deal with disobedience. In violation of the Law, the returnees had allowed Tobiah, an Ammonite, use of a room in the temple. In addition, the people stopped supporting the Levites who served in the temple and also were illegally working and selling on the Sabbath. Nehemiah ordered the Levites to guard the city's entrances and threatened to arrest anyone who tried to bring merchandise into it on the Sabbath.

Also, like Ezra, Nehemiah discovered that some Jews had married Gentile wives who worshiped other gods. For the same reasons, Nehemiah required the same drastic solution. He commanded those who'd married foreign wives to separate from them.

New Testament

The work and reforms of Nehemiah have two significant implications for the New Testament.

First, once again, his emphasis on ethnic purity was imperative for preserving the hearts and the lineage of the Jewish people.

Second, his concern and passion for Jerusalem highlights the city's centrality in the history of Israel and the future of the church.

After capturing it, David made Jerusalem, originally a Jebusite fortress, the religious and political capital of all Israel by moving the ark of the covenant there. Jerusalem served as Judah's political capital and religious center until the Babylonians destroyed it and looted the temple (586 BC).

Under the leadership of Zerubbabel, the Jews rebuilt Jerusalem and the temple. After their enemies apparently destroyed part of the city and burned its walls, Nehemiah organized their full reconstruction.

From the post-exilic period to the time of Christ, Jerusalem was Israel's symbol of national identity. During his ministry, Jesus visited Jerusalem at least three times to celebrate Passover. Jesus made his triumphal entry into the city, wept over the city, predicted its destruction, and was crucified outside of it.

Jerusalem was a key location for the first-century church. Jesus told his followers to stay there until they received the gift of the Holy Spirit, and then they were to be his witnesses beginning at Jerusalem and expanding out to Judea, Samaria, and the whole world. The church, born in Jerusalem, initially worshiped in the temple and met in homes. Stephen was martyred in Jerusalem. The first church council met there to resolve the attempt by Jewish believers to impose the Mosaic Covenant on Gentile converts.

Though Jerusalem was initially the sending church, the church at Antioch became the sender for the mission to the Gentiles. Still, Paul never forgot about his Jewish countrymen. While on his second missionary journey, he made the decision to go both to Jerusalem and Rome (before being arrested in Jerusalem and later transferred to Caesarea).

The Romans totally destroyed Jerusalem in AD 70 and later would prohibit any Jew from setting foot in the city on penalty of death.

In fulfillment of the Lord's promises to his people, Christ promised to return to Jerusalem and rescue a repentant Jewish remnant. In Revelation, John described the eternal home for God's people as the New Jerusalem.

Jesus and the Samaritans

In the time of Jesus, his encounter with the Samaritan woman reflects the centuries-old mutual hostility. When he and his disciples traveled north from Judea to Galilee, they took the direct route through Samaria. Most Jews took a longer route in order to avoid it altogether.

When they reached the village of Sychar, Jesus went to a well and asked for a drink. Shocked, the woman said, "You are a Jew, and I am a Samaritan woman. Why are you asking me for a drink?" (John 4:9 NLT). Jews considered Samaritans "fools" and used Samaritan as a racial slur to criticize Jesus. When he asked about her husband, she sought to change the subject because she'd been married five times: "The woman said to Him, 'Sir, I perceive that You are a prophet. Our fathers worshiped in this mountain, and you people say that in Jerusalem is the place where men ought to worship'" (4:19–20 NASB). She was referring to Mount Gerizim, where the Samaritans had built the rival temple. Jesus' answer focused on the nature, not the place, of worship: "God is spirit, and those who worship Him must worship in spirit and truth" (v. 24 NASB).

The Origin of the Samaritans

After Israel's King Omri made Samaria his capital, the name was sometimes used for the whole northern kingdom. The Assyrians conquered it in 722 BC and deported most of the Israelites, then resettled Israel with conquered peoples from other nations. Over time the remaining Israelites intermarried with the foreigners and combined worship of the Lord with worship of the gods the relocated settlers had served. This racially and religiously mixed group were called Samaritans.

Realizing that his disciples were not yet prepared to cross this racial boundary, Jesus prohibited them from ministering to Samaritans during his earthly life (Matthew 10:5–7). Once, when he was on his way to Jerusalem, Samaritans refused to let him enter their village (Luke 9:52–53).

However, in his gospel, Luke includes Samaritans among the outcasts Jesus loved. When Jesus healed ten lepers, only the Samaritan leper returned to thank him (17:11–19). When an expert in Jewish law (a scribe) asked, "Who is my neighbor?" Jesus answered with the parable of the Good Samaritan (10:19–37). After thieves beat and robbed a man traveling from Jerusalem to Jericho, neither a Jewish priest nor a Levite stopped to help him. Instead, a despised Samaritan treated his wounds and paid for him to have a room in an inn and care until he recovered.

After the resurrection, Jesus noted Samaria as a distinct geographical and ethnic location in directing his followers to bring the good news "in Jerusalem, and in all Judea and Samaria, and to the ends of the earth" (Acts 1:8).

Philip and the Samaritans

Philip was the first Christian to minister in Samaria (Acts 8). Due to the enmity between Jews and Samaritans, his ministry was groundbreaking and courageous. Luke says simply that Philip preached Christ. Many Samaritans believed and were baptized; however, contrary to the "normative conversion pattern" in Acts, they did not receive the Holy Spirit when they believed.

When the Jewish church in Jerusalem heard about this, they sent Peter and John to investigate. After the apostles arrived and discovered the deficiency, they gave the Samaritans the gift of the Spirit through the laying on of hands (vv. 12–17). This two-stage conversion experience served to confirm the unity in Christ between Jewish and Samaritan believers.

Conclusion

Up to the exile, Israel had functioned primarily as a nation under a theocratic ruler, a divinely appointed king. Now it was a Persian province administered by an appointed governor. As a result, the people lost their national identity and placed more emphasis on their identity as individuals. But the prophets continued to emphasize God's faithfulness and inspire hope for the future.

In addition to fueling hope, the prophets highlighted an expanded concept (a further revelation) of God. That the Lord was sovereign over all the earth—all its nations and peoples—was a specific exilic-prophetic emphasis. The book of Daniel reveals a panorama of history to come that focuses on God's universal rule.

The exile also helped cure Israel of idolatry. Apostasy was one of its primary causes; Israel had abandoned the Lord and worshiped the idols and spirits of other nations. After the exile, the Jews would become fervent monotheists (worshipers of one god).

Though some exile-related changes were positive, some were devastating to the spiritual dynamic of God's people. Instead of observing the Law of Moses out of love and devotion for the Lord, for many, law-keeping became empty ritualism. Many (though not all) turned the Law upside down; they thought keeping it was a way to earn God's favor and used it as an ethnic marker to distinguish themselves from (and over) Gentiles. Malachi, in the Old Testament's last book, sternly warned about the dangers of hypocritical ceremonialism. He guaranteed that a divine messenger was coming as a refining fire and fullers' soap (a strong detergent), and he reminded them that the Lord wanted his people to be honest, compassionate, and just (3:1–5 NASB).

Questions for Discussion

1. Read Isaiah 44:28 and Ezra 1:1–2 and discuss how God used Cyrus to bring the Jews back to Israel. What does

the return from exile reveal about God's sovereignty over history?

2. Do you agree with what the Jews decided in refusing the Samaritans' offer to help rebuild the temple? Why or why not?

3. Discuss (a) the function of the synagogue for the Jews in exile and (b) the relevance of the synagogue for the ministries of Jesus and Paul.

4. While the local church is not a synagogue, discuss its role in education and in the promotion of a Christian lifestyle.

5. In what ways was Jesus' ministering to the woman at the well so radical? What did his actions and words reveal about the love of God? What are some contemporary situations that might be similar to how Jesus connected with her?

6. Regarding Philip's work in Samaria, why was there an ethnic and cultural barrier to ministry there? Discuss one more situation that relates to the contemporary church's difficulty in ministering to the various ethnic groups.

2

Alexander the Great: The Apostle of Hellenism

The Greek Period

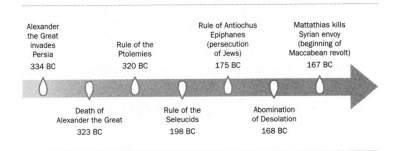

Alexander the Great invades Persia
334 BC

Rule of the Ptolemies
320 BC

Rule of Antiochus Epiphanes (persecution of Jews)
175 BC

Mattathias kills Syrian envoy (beginning of Maccabean revolt)
167 BC

Death of Alexander the Great
323 BC

Rule of the Seleucids
198 BC

Abomination of Desolation
168 BC

Introduction

(337 BC: Alexander, son of the king of Macedonia, is a student of Aristotle.)

Aristotle was proud of his best pupil. That the young Alexander was diligent and bright was not surprising. He was the son of King Philip of Macedonia, and while studying under Aristotle, he became convinced that the Greek way of life was far superior to any other. (It is recorded that he carried both the *Iliad* and the *Odyssey* on his military campaigns.)

He was destined to become Alexander the Great, "the apostle of Hellenism."

Philip had unified the Macedonians into a potent military state. Under his leadership, the former peasants and shepherds had become an extremely skilled and highly mobile fighting force. After he had subdued the Greek city-states, Philip planned to conquer Asia; however, his dream of conquest ended abruptly when he was assassinated at a banquet in 337 BC.

The Empire of Alexander

Alexander was a brilliant military strategist with a love for learning. He was only twenty when his father was murdered, yet he had inherited both a small empire and Philip's military genius. In addition to his highly trained troops, he incorporated historians, geographers, and botanists into his army. He not only planned to conquer other nations, he also wanted to establish centers of learning to indoctrinate people in the Greek way of life.

Alexander followed through on the dream when he entered Asia Minor in 334 BC by crossing the narrow Hellespont (now called the Dardanelles). Darius III of Persia sent a small force to stop him but had badly underestimated the strength of the Macedonian army. Though he was almost killed, Alexander defeated the Persians at the Granicus River.

When Alexander continued advancing to the east, Darius engaged him again at Issus. Again the Macedonians prevailed, and the Persians retreated. Alexander made a surprise attack on Damascus, capturing the city and the family of Darius. Darius attempted to negotiate a treaty, but Alexander refused. He had determined to surmount the world.

Alexander advanced south, capturing Tyre and threatening Jerusalem. Josephus, a historian from the Roman period, later said that when Alexander threatened to destroy Jerusalem and the temple, the high priest Jaddua met him and read passages from the book of Daniel that predicted his victory over the Persians. Alexander was so impressed that he exempted the Jews from paying tribute and permitted them to live according to their own laws. According to Josephus, some Jews even joined his army. These intriguing accounts suggest an openness to Hellenism by some Jews in order to preserve their traditions (*Antiquities of the Jews* 11.8.4–5).

After capturing Gaza, Alexander entered Egypt. The Egyptians despised the Persians, who occupied their country, and welcomed him as their liberator.

Alexander could be ruthless, but he was not a cruel dictator. He knew the importance of winning the support of those he conquered. He worshiped at Egyptian temples and allowed the Egyptians to govern their country. They made him a Pharaoh and worshiped him as a god.

To promote Hellenism, he established the city of Alexandria. "The jewel of the East" became a major commercial and educational center. Over time large numbers of Jews settled there and developed an "Alexandrian Judaism" that was a synthesis of Hellenistic and Jewish culture and philosophy.

At this time hostilities between Jews and Samaritans were made worse when the Samaritans rebelled against—and burned alive—their Macedonian governor. Alexander put

---

* This reference, later abbreviated *Ant.*, refers to a twenty-volume work composed by the Jewish historian Flavius Josephus around AD 93.

down the revolt and destroyed the city of Shechem. For their help, he rewarded the Jews by giving them more territory in Samaria, but he also allowed the Samaritans to build a temple on Mount Gerizim.

Though Alexander accepted his divine-deliverer status, he had not given up on world conquest. He remained in Egypt only a little over a year, then led his army north through Israel and Syria to defeat the Persians completely.

The two armies met at Gaugamela in Mesopotamia. Though the Persians significantly outnumbered the Macedonians, the forces of Darius were routed. He escaped, yet now there was nothing to stop Alexander from seizing control of the vast Persian Empire.

Moving east, Alexander captured the cities of Babylon, Susa, Persepolis, and Ecbatana. He led his armies even further through Afghanistan and into India. But after three more years of campaigns, he was forced back to Persia. His Macedonian soldiers refused to go any farther; they wanted to go home.

While Alexander had believed the Greek way of life was matchless, his passion for Hellenism nonetheless was corrupted by the seductive appeal of Oriental culture. He began to dress and rule like an Oriental king. He married Roxana, a Bactrian princess, and bribed thousands of officers and soldiers to marry Persian wives. When he made Persians generals, his Macedonian officers protested, and he had to put down a rebellion within his own ranks.

Emperor worship was common in the East, and the Egyptians had honored Alexander as a god. While Greek mythology told stories about divine rulers, the Greeks debated whether or not Alexander was a living deity. Though never a significant movement, the cult of Alexander set precedence for the future development of emperor worship in the West. Ironically, Alexander's death resulted not from battle but from disease. He died in ancient Babylon from malaria or possibly alcoholism at age thirty-two. It had only been eleven years since he'd left Greece and crossed into Asia Minor, but he had established one of the world's largest empires.

Alexander was dead; his dream, however, was not. In each conquered land he'd established a model Hellenistic city. He was convinced that when people discovered Greek culture, they'd recognize it as a superior way to live, to be, and enthusiastically adopt it. And, to some extent, he was right. In his educational centers, people studied Greek philosophy and language. The administration of cities was modeled after Greek city-states, and citizens adopted Greek dress. Greek became the vast empire's common language.

The Division of Alexander's Empire

Certainly Alexander's demise had been unexpected. Now his only son, born *after* his death, was too young to rule. His generals struggled to gain control for seven years, and eventually the empire was divided among four of them:

- Antigonus had the largest area, from the Mediterranean to Central Asia (including northern Syria)
- Cassander was in charge of Macedonia
- Lysimachus controlled Thrace
- Ptolemy ruled Egypt and southern Syria (*Ant.* 12.1.1)

Antigonus aspired to become a second Alexander. But when he declared himself king, the other generals declared war on him. He was killed in battle against Lysimachus, Cassander, and Seleucus, who was Ptolemy's general. Because Ptolemy himself had not joined the others against Antigonus, they rewarded Seleucus with Antigonus's territories; Ptolemy retained control of Egypt and of the regions of "southern Syria," which by the boundaries they'd drawn up for themselves included the land that had belonged to Israel.

The Jews' Promised Land, now known as Palestine, was both militarily and economically strategic *and* surrounded by two powerful empires. Ptolemy wanted it as a military buffer against invasion of Egypt from the north; Seleucus valued its natural resources and its key trade routes to the east.

The Ptolemies and the Jews (Israel)

(The primary source for information on the rule of the Ptolemies and Seleucids is from Josephus, *Ant.* 12.1–5.)

Palestine came under Ptolemaic/Egyptian rule when Ptolemy I (known as *Soter*; r. 323–285 BC) invaded and easily captured Jerusalem because the Jews refused to fight on the Sabbath. He reportedly deported 100,000 to Egypt, which partially accounts for a large Jewish population there. Ptolemy did not force Hellenistic rule and culture on Palestine, allowing the Jews to live according to their traditions. They were free to observe the Law, and the high priest was responsible for governing.

Like most ancient rulers, though, Ptolemy exploited conquered nations. He set up a taxation system in Palestine, and local collectors were required to pay a tax quota from their district. The revenue was sent to Egypt, not used to benefit the taxpayers. Local officials could extort more than the required quota from those in their district and keep the surplus for themselves. Famously, the Romans used a similar system when they later occupied Palestine.

During the rule of Ptolemy II (*Philadelphus*; son of Ptolemy I; r. 285–246 BC), Alexandrian Jews completed a translation of the Old Testament that became the official version for both Diaspora Jews (living away from Palestine) and Palestinian Jews. The *Letter of Aristeas* (c. 100 BC) gives a fascinating account of the process. An official of Ptolemy Philadelphus supposedly urged him to start a library at Alexandria. He'd become interested in Jewish law, so he recruited Eleazar, high priest in Jerusalem, to translate the Old Testament from Hebrew into Greek so a copy could be in the library. Eleazar allegedly sent seventy-two exceptional elders to Alexandria. The *Letter of Aristeas* says that, working independently in separate rooms, they produced identical Greek translations in seventy-two days. (In some versions, the number of translators *and* the days of translation are seventy. Thus, the standard abbreviation for the Septuagint is LXX [Roman numeral 70]).

The Seleucids and the Jews (Israel)

Unable to keep control over Mesopotamia in the East, the Seleucids (as the rulers of the empire of Seleucus became known) moved their capital from Babylon to northern Syria, on the Mediterranean, and named the new capital Antioch, after the Seleucid ruler Antiochus II.

For a quarter century the Seleucids (Syria) fought the Ptolemies (Egypt) for control of Palestine. The Ptolemies never won a decisive victory, but they maintained control until Ptolemy IV (*Philopater*; r. 221–203 BC) died. His son was only five years old; now Egypt was thrown into a chaotic power struggle. The Seleucids finally had their opportunity.

Antiochus III (or Antiochus the Great; r. 223–187 BC) invaded Palestine and won the decisive conflict at Panium, near the headwaters of the Jordan River. The Egyptian general Scopas retreated from the battlefield and then later surrendered. In 198 BC, Palestine came under Seleucid rule.

Still, Antiochus the Great was not the only one forging and furthering an empire. The Romans were expanding to the east; they'd already conquered several cities in Greece. And Antiochus made a costly mistake when he invaded and engaged them there (190 BC). After he was defeated, he was forced not only to pay tribute but also (for insurance that he would keep his obligations) to send his son Antiochus IV to Rome as a hostage. When the elder Antiochus died three years later, Seleucus IV succeeded him (and kept paying heavy tribute, which he managed only by taxing his subjects more heavily, including the Jews).

The younger Antiochus spent a dozen years in Rome before at last being allowed to return to Syria. There he served for a time as an official under Seleucus IV. Then he murdered the king and seized the throne for himself.

Antiochus IV now ruled the Seleucid Empire, yet he inherited the same (and worsening) problem of continually needing to acquire sufficient resources to hand over to Rome so as—hopefully—to keep *that* increasingly growing and strengthening empire from seeking to swallow up his.

The Hellenization of Israel

Fast-forward a few years. A messenger had come from Rome to Antioch, the Seleucid capital, bearing news. When he read the edict, King Antiochus IV was outraged. The Romans were demanding even *more* tribute.

Antiochus knew he had no choice—he had to pay what Rome required. He had learned, as a hostage, that Rome would not tolerate insubordination.

When Antiochus (r. 175–163 BC) took over, he'd given himself the name *Epiphanes*, "the Manifest One" (as in, "manifestation" of a god). He was driven by arrogance; further, though, he was passionate for the spread and ultimate triumph of Greek culture. Unlike the Ptolemies, who hadn't forced the Jews to adopt Greek ways, Antiochus was determined to Hellenize his subjects—and no one more so than the Jews, whom he hated. He would demand that they abandon Judaism and conform, persecuting dissenters with tactics so merciless and brutal that they would lead to the Jewish fight for independence.

For the moment, Antiochus faced a very specific crisis. Rome wanted *more* tribute? The solution was simple: increased taxation on the Jews.

Antiochus Epiphanes and the Abomination of Desolation

Some Jews did adopt Greek customs and support Syrian rule. Opposed to them most fervently, in a domestic sense, were traditionalists who tenaciously held to orthodox Jewish customs; these became known as *Hasidim*, "pious ones" (1 Maccabees 2:29–38, 42–44). The Hasidim later divided into groups (or parties) known as the Pharisees and the Essenes (see chapters 4 and 8).

Jewish supporters of Hellenism aside, the relationship between the Jews and Syrians deteriorated precipitously and thoroughly under the egomaniacal tyrant-king. For his tyranny, the Jews already had nicknamed him Antiochus *Epimanes* ("madman," a play upon *Epiphanes*). Now they realized he considered the office of high priest a political position and was willing to sell it to the highest bidder. Traditional Jews held the priesthood to be of lifelong duration, and regarded the high priest to be their spiritual leader.

Onias III, an orthodox Jew, lost the office to his brother Jason, a Hellenist, when Jason offered Antiochus a huge bribe. Then Jason sought to transform Jerusalem into a Greek city-state, establishing a Hellenistic school and building a gymnasium for athletic contests in which Jewish young men participated in the nude. Some even underwent surgery to hide the evidence of circumcision. Orthodox Jews were scandalized.

Jason would become a victim of his own sort of intrigue. Menelaus, from the tribe of Benjamin (not in the priestly line), bought the office, also by bribing Antiochus, and then tried to assassinate Jason, who was forced to flee Jerusalem. This treachery was so contemptible that many Jews who'd been willing to make concessions to the Hellenists changed their minds. The Hasidim began to organize a resistance movement.

Menelaus used the temple treasury to bribe his friends and pay taxes to Antiochus. When the former high priest Onias moved to tell Antiochus of these offenses, Menelaus had him murdered. When the Jews in Jerusalem found out Menelaus was robbing the temple, they rioted. Menelaus unleashed Syrian soldiers, and many Jews were killed.

Jason, though a fugitive in exile, had not given up on returning as high priest. He organized a small army east of the Jordan River, and when Antiochus was on a campaign in Egypt, attacked and occupied Jerusalem. Frustrated when he was unable to kill Menelaus, who'd barricaded himself in a fortress, Jason turned on the citizens.

When Antiochus heard of this, he sent his troops to quell the rebellion. Jason and his thousand mercenaries were scattered, and hundreds of orthodox Jews—men, women, and children—were slaughtered. The temple was looted, and Menelaus was restored as high priest. Realizing to a greater extent the feelings and views of many Jews, Antiochus now stationed an occupying force in Jerusalem to keep Menelaus in power and to enforce his policies.

In 168 BC, Antiochus made another bid to gain control over Egypt and would have succeeded had Rome not intervened. The senate sent a general to warn him against further expansion. When Pompillus intercepted Antiochus near Alexandria and ordered him out of Egypt, Antiochus said he'd consider the request. That was insufficient for Pompillus, who drew a circle in the sand around Antiochus and demanded an answer before he stepped from it.

Antiochus was helpless. From personal experience, he knew that defiance would compel Rome to crush his empire. He withdrew.

Humiliated and enraged, the "madman" then launched a campaign of terror to eradicate traditional Judaism. He ordered everyone in the empire to worship Greek deities. He demanded that Jews abandon their own customs and adopt the Greek lifestyle. He imposed the death penalty on anyone who practiced circumcision, observed the Sabbath or other

"Abomination That Causes Desolation"

In 167 BC, Antiochus Epiphanes set up an idol to Zeus on the temple's altar of burnt offering and sacrificed unclean animals (Daniel 9:26–27; cf. 11:31; 12:11). In his Olivet Discourse, Jesus looked back on this as a foreshadowing of a future "abomination of desolation" (Matthew 24:15; Mark 13:14). Some think he was referring to Jerusalem's destruction in AD 70 by Titus and his legions, or the shocking occupation of the temple by Jewish zealots prior to the Roman invasion. (Titus's soldiers also set up idols and sacrificed to their gods.) Others interpret Jesus' words as referring to a temple desecration by "the man of lawlessness" (the Antichrist) during a future period of tribulation (2 Thessalonians 2:3–4). Christians should be cautious about insisting on a dogmatic interpretation.

Jewish religious festivals, or even possessed a copy of the Scriptures. Eleazar, an older scribe, was flogged to death for refusing to eat pork. Other Jews were tortured and killed for refusing to worship Zeus.

Antiochus caused the most heinous offense when he attacked on the Sabbath and his army occupied Jerusalem. They destroyed the walls built by Nehemiah and built a fortress called the Akra. In contempt for Judaism, Greek soldiers indulged in drunken orgies in the temple courts. They desecrated the temple by erecting an altar to Zeus in the Holy of Holies and sacrificing pigs and other unclean animals on the altar. Daniel had foretold this monstrous event, known as "the Abomination of Desolation" (ref. Daniel 11:31).

Instead of destroying Jewish will to resist Hellenism, the odious sacrilege ignited a revolution that began in Modin, a small village to the northwest.

The Impact of Hellenism on the Jews

Alexander was a military conqueror *and* a cultural warrior, convinced of the Greek way of life's superiority and certain that conquered peoples would recognize Hellenism's advantages once exposed to them. Moving to the east, he established educational centers with courses on language, commerce, government, philosophy, and the arts. Hellenism flourished in some places, such as Alexandria (Egypt), which became a prominent Greek city-state with one of the ancient world's largest and most influential educational centers. Greek became the language of commerce. People wore Greek dress, attended athletic contests that deified Greek gods, and studied Greek philosophy.

But to what extent did Greek language and culture impact Judaism? All Jews were influenced to some extent, yet the New Testament distinguishes between Palestinian (or "Hebraic," see NIV) and Hellenistic Jews (Acts 6:1). Though Jews who lived in Palestine spoke Greek, they were resistant to Hellenistic changes and insisted on preserving traditional practices. On the other hand, Hellenistic or Diaspora Jews (those who lived elsewhere in the Mediterranean world) synthesized traditional Judaism with Greek thought and culture. For an insightful biblical example, consider Peter and Paul. Peter lived in Palestine and clung tenaciously to traditional practices (e.g., see Acts 10, regarding Peter and Cornelius, a Gentile). Paul, from Tarsus (a city in southern Asia Minor, now Turkey), was able to minister effectively to Gentiles all over because he was comfortable in a Hellenistic environment.

The book of Acts records two specific situations that illustrate Paul's effectiveness in this arena. When the church in Jerusalem sent Barnabas to Antioch to see about the Gentile response to the gospel, he found that many had become believers. Instead of requesting help with the ministry from the Jewish church in Jerusalem, he sent for Paul, who had recently trusted Christ as Savior (Acts 10). Barnabas knew that as a Hellenistic Jew Paul was more capable for ministry to Gentiles than Palestinian Jews.

Also, when Paul arrived in Athens, he was distressed by rampant idolatry there, but instead of condemning the Athenians, he drew on his knowledge of Greek philosophy to skillfully contextualize the gospel to the Epicureans and Stoics. Using the altar "to an unknown god" (Acts 17:23) as a point of contact, he proclaimed that there is one true God, the creator and sustainer of life, and that His Son, risen from the dead, will one day judge all. Though they mocked Paul for his claim of the resurrection, his Hellenistic training (he even quoted a Greek poet, v. 28) enabled him to challenge their philosophical beliefs.

The Greek Language and the Septuagint

Greek was the official language in the territories Alexander's successors controlled. Jews, like other conquered peoples, were forced to speak it to live and work in a Hellenistic environment. For many outside Palestine, Greek became the primary language, and this probably was the case with Paul. On his journeys, when he spoke in synagogues and cited the Old Testament, all the quotes are from the Greek Septuagint rather than the Hebrew text.

Comparison of the Old Testament texts quoted in the New Testament yields an amazing discovery. They are similar but not identical to the Hebrew Old Testament. The New Testament writers apparently used the Septuagint as their Old Testament source, which would make sense if the majority of Jews and Gentiles spoke Greek. Matthew was a tax collector before he became a disciple; Luke was a physician. Both would have had a formal education and been competent in Greek. In fact, the language style in Luke's gospel is more like classical Greek than the *koine* (common) Greek that most people spoke.

Today, scholars use the Septuagint to clarify the meaning of difficult Old Testament passages. The classic example is Isaiah 7:14, where the Hebrew word *almah* refers to a young girl of marriageable age and not specifically to one who is a virgin. But the Septuagint translates Isaiah 7:14 with *parthenos*, which is used only for a woman who is a virgin, and Matthew (1:23) quotes the Septuagint.

Antioch and Christianity

Antioch, which had been the Seleucid capital, was an important city for the early church's growth. When persecution forced believers from Jerusalem, some went as far as Antioch and preached the gospel to Greeks. Many believed, and the Jerusalem church sent Barnabas to teach the converts. He recruited Paul to help, and the two men ministered together there for a year. Believers were first called *Christians* at Antioch, and its church eventually replaced the Jerusalem church for the mission to Gentiles (Acts 10:19–26).

Though Jerusalem was originally Christianity's center of growth, the church at Antioch became Paul's base for missionary activity. The Hellenistic Christians there were more motivated for and open to preaching the gospel to Gentiles than were the early Jewish Christians in Jerusalem. Under the Holy Spirit's direction, the church at Antioch commissioned Paul and Barnabas for the first missionary journey, and after each of his next two journeys Paul returned there before departing again (15:36; 18:22–23).

As a result of that first journey, large numbers of Gentiles had become Christians. This alarmed a group of Jewish traditionalists from Judea, and they traveled to Antioch demanding that Gentile believers undergo circumcision to mark them as Jews. Both Paul and Barnabas vehemently objected to imposing a Jewish ritual on Gentiles for salvation.

The elders in the Antioch church sent them and others to Jerusalem to resolve the issue. After discussing the problem, the church at Jerusalem agreed with Paul and Barnabas that Gentiles were saved by grace, just as Jews were. The Jerusalem church sent a letter informing Antioch of their decision, a decision that greatly encouraged the Antioch church because it preserved unity between Gentile and Jewish believers and did not impose a requirement on Gentiles that would have made evangelism difficult (Acts 15). The Jerusalem Council's ruling made it possible for the Hellenistic church at Antioch to continue as a base for the church's outreach to Gentiles.

The Antioch Church vs. Alexandrian Allegorism

Jews in Alexandria faced a dilemma. Greek thought fascinated them, yet they didn't want to abandon Judaism. To harmonize the Old Testament with Greek philosophy, they adopted an allegorical means of interpreting Scripture.

Greek philosophers used the allegorical method to resolve the moral and ethical dilemma created by stories of the drunkenness and sexual immorality of the Greek gods. Herein the tales should not be interpreted literally but allegorically—the real meaning is hidden behind the "historical" narrative. Using allegory, the divine debauchery instead focused epic tales on the struggle between good and evil.

Around 160 BC, Aristobulus, an Alexandrian Jew, taught that the Old Testament was the source for Greek philosophical ideas. For Philo (c. 20 BC–AD 50), the most famous of these allegorists, Scripture's true meaning was the "hidden" meaning behind the literal meaning—thus, the story of Abraham was of a Greek philosopher in search of wisdom. Through allegory he was able to harmonize the parts of the Old Testament that offended the Greeks.

Hermeneutics were different at Antioch, where Christian interpreters rejected such application of allegory and held tenaciously to the literal approach to interpretation. It is possible that the Antioch church insisted on the preeminence of this method through Paul's influence (see above, under "Antioch and Christianity").

The Sanhedrin and Jesus

When Jesus began his ministry, the Sanhedrin became suspicious of his miracles and teaching. In Jerusalem for the Feast

The Sanhedrin

The Jewish Sanhedrin's origin is uncertain; some say it was modeled after legislative councils in Greek city-states (*sanhedrin* is Greek for "assembly"), but it may have had Old Testament origins. Precedent for a council of seventy members might have come after the exodus, when God summoned Moses, Aaron, Nadab, Abihu, and seventy elders to approach him on Mount Sinai (Exodus 24:1). Later, while each city with a sizable Jewish population had its own "sanhedrin," the seventy-elder council (plus the high priest) in Jerusalem became the supreme legislative authority and was called "the Great Sanhedrin."

The high council gained legislative power as a result of Greek influence. In Judea, the Sanhedrin served as both a civil and religious court. Its members were Pharisees, Sadducees, and scribes; the high priest presided. Law-breakers could be flogged, excommunicated, or in extreme cases, executed by stoning. Under Roman rule, the Sanhedrin could not impose the death penalty, so after it condemned Jesus, he was brought to the Roman governor. When Pilate first refused to examine him, the Jews noted, "We have no right to execute anyone" (John 18:31). Even so, when the council found Stephen guilty of blasphemy against God and Moses, he was assaulted, dragged from the city, and stoned (Acts 7:54–60). Regarding religious complaints, it seems the Romans allowed the imposition of capital punishment (or at least ignored executions related to violations of Mosaic Law).

of Tabernacles, they took his claim that God was his Father to be so outrageous that the high priest decided on strong action: They threatened to expel from the synagogue anyone who listened to his teaching (John 7:12–13). They learned that people were already talking about him, so they sent the temple police to arrest him (v. 32), who also were captivated by his teaching and returned empty-handed (v. 44).

Not all council members rejected Jesus as an imposter. Nicodemus was amazed by his miracles and came to him in the darkness of night (3:1–15). He was shocked, misunderstanding, when Jesus said he would never enter God's kingdom unless he experienced a spiritual transformation as miraculous as birth, but he didn't condemn him as a false prophet. At the feast, when the Pharisees charged that Jesus was an imposter, Nicodemus defended him (7:37–53). And after Jesus had been crucified, Nicodemus helped Joseph of Arimathea with the burial arrangements for his body (19:38–42).

After Jesus raised Lazarus, the high priest Caiaphas called for a meeting of the Sanhedrin. Fearing Jesus' popularity with the people would alarm the Romans, who might then destroy the nation, he convinced the council that Jesus should be put to death (11:45–53). They bribed Judas to betray Jesus (Matthew 26:14–16), then tried and condemned him (John 22:66–71).

The Sanhedrin and the Early Church

The Sanhedrin's opposition to Jesus and his followers did not end there. In fact, his death and resurrection *fueled* opposition from the council because of the church's explosive growth. When Peter and John claimed they'd healed a handicapped man in Jesus' name and thousands joined the church, the high council had them arrested. They threatened Peter and John, and ordered them to stop teaching the people that Jesus was alive, but could not convict them because of the miraculous healing of the lame man (Acts 4:1–22).

Believers continued to preach the gospel, so the Sanhedrin ordered all the apostles arrested, but an angel released them (5:1–42). They were seized again and brought to trial, and because they refused to obey the Sanhedrin, they were flogged and released. Stephen, a deacon charged with blasphemy and tried before the Sanhedrin, was stoned to death for claiming that Jesus was the promised Messiah and that they were mistaken in rejecting him (6:8–7:60).

After the Romans in Jerusalem arrested Paul on suspicion of causing a riot, an officer gave him permission to speak to the Sanhedrin. When Paul saw he would not get a fair hearing, he brought up the issue of the resurrection, sparking violent debate between the Pharisees and Sadducees (22:30–23:11).

The Sanhedrin was so determined to get rid of Paul that they conspired with a group of fanatical assassins to kill him (23:12–22). When the Romans transferred him to Caesarea to protect him, the high priest and a delegation from the Sanhedrin along with an attorney came to present their case before the Roman governor (24:1–9).

Questions for Discussion

1. Discuss the positive and negative impacts of Alexander's conquests and the spread of Hellenism in the world of Jesus.

2. How did events in the city of Alexandria help prepare the world for Jesus' coming?

3. What were some differences between a Palestinian Jew and a Hellenistic Jew? Discuss why Hellenistic Jewish believers were better suited for ministry to Gentiles.

4. Discuss the importance of Antioch for the growth of the church. Why do you think the church there became the sending church for Paul's missionary journeys?

5. Discuss what you believe to be the historic (past) and prophetic (future) significance of the "Abomination of Desolation."

3

A Courageous Priest and His Sons

The Maccabean Revolt

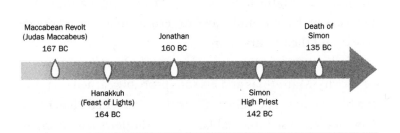

Maccabean Revolt
(Judas Maccabeus)
167 BC

Jonathan
160 BC

Death of
Simon
135 BC

Hanakkuh
(Feast of Lights)
164 BC

Simon
High Priest
142 BC

Introduction

(167 BC: Palestine is under Syrian rule as part of the Seleucid Empire.)

"Mattathias! *Mattathias!* Where's Mattathias!" called the breathless messenger. He'd raced to the village of Modin with appalling news and now found the priest at home, with his five sons.

(Primary sources on the Maccabean Revolt: Josephus, *Antiquities* 12.6–14.4; 1 and 2 Maccabees, books of Jewish history from the Apochrypha)

Mattathias welcomed the young man and offered him food and water. "Tell me," he said. "What has happened?"

"Something *terrible*," the man moaned. "The Syrians have defiled the temple. *Soldiers* occupied the Holy Place—they put up an altar to Zeus in the *Holy of Holies*. And they sacrificed a *pig* on the altar.

"The high priest is heartbroken. He has called this 'the Abomination of Desolation.' And Mattathias, the Hasidim are outraged—they're organizing for war. They now have said they'll fight to the death to stop the oppression."

For temple service, the priests were organized into twenty-four divisions. Each division served only two weeks annually, so many, like Mattathias, chose to live in villages a short distance away. They would travel to Jerusalem for their service weeks and then return home.

Modin was about twenty miles (one day's walk) northwest of the city. Mattathias and his sons probably earned their living by farming. The "Greeks" (as the Jews called Hellenistic Gentiles) despised manual labor, but the Jews traditionally valued work as service to God. One of a father's duties was to teach his son a trade.

Mattathias felt torn up inside. Soon it would be his turn to serve, but how could he sacrifice to the Lord where pagans had defiled? The Syrians were monsters—something had to be done. What could they do? What could *he* do?

Before long another messenger came to Modin. The Seleucid envoy of King Antiochus IV, known as "Epiphanes" (or *Epipmanes*—see chapter 2), demanded that all Jews renounce their God and sacrifice to a Greek god.

The man had an altar set up in the center of the village. After summoning the inhabitants, who'd slowly congregated, he barked at Mattathias: "*You!* Old priest! Set an example for us. Step forward, and sacrifice—to your *new* god."

Mattathias's blood froze.

His neighbors stared, horrified. What *would* he do?

Then his blood began to boil. The aged man set his chin, straightened his back, and began to speak, loudly and sternly. "Hear, O Israel, the Lord our God, the Lord is *one*! Even if you—even if all others—abandon him and worship the king's idol, my sons and I will worship *only* God."

For a moment, hearts swelled. The villagers were amazed at his courage.

But then one younger man stepped forward. He began to march toward the altar. As he approached it became clear he planned to sacrifice.

He never made it. Mattathias drew his sacrificial knife, lunged out, and slew the apostate. Then he killed the Syrian emissary also.

With his sons, along with other zealous Jews, Mattathias fled into the Judean wilderness. The revolt had begun.

Freedom Fighters

From all over the land, other bands of rebels joined the original group. At first, however, the movement was disorganized and lacked a fighting strategy.

One significant issue was that the day sacred to the Jews, the one devoted to the Lord, meant nothing to the "Greeks." When a Syrian detachment found a group of Jews hiding in the hills on the Sabbath, the soldiers advanced on their position, the Jews refused to fight, and a thousand men, women, and children were slaughtered. When the rebels heard about the disaster, they decided that no matter when their foe attacked they would fight to the death, but they would never initiate an assault on the Sabbath.

Mattathias, elderly when the insurgency began, soon died of natural causes. Beforehand, he chose his oldest son, Judas, to lead the revolt. Judas earned the nickname *Maccabeus,* from a word for "hammer," because he dealt the Syrians a series of hammer-like blows. The rebels were called the Maccabees, and the uprising became known as the Maccabean Revolt.

Antiochus, facing more than one threat to his empire, took half his army to stop an invasion in the East. Lysias, his minister of state, organized the other half to destroy the revolutionaries. The Syrians, so confident of victory that they hired slave traders to sell Jews to other nations, underestimated the courage and determination of the outnumbered Maccabees.

For instance, while camped at the town of Emmaus, the Syrians divided their numbers and sent a small unit to search for Judas. When he learned their army was split, he led a surprise attack that became a rout. They burned the whole camp; the other Syrian force fled when they saw their base in flames.

After that defeat, the Syrians sent sixty thousand hand-picked infantry and five thousand cavalry to find and destroy the rebels. Before Judas engaged this superior force with only ten thousand soldiers, he prayed,

All praise to the Savior of Israel, who helped David defeat the giant and Israel the Philistines. Overthrow our enemies by the sword of those who love you, and let all who know you praise your name with songs of thanksgiving. (1 Maccabees 4:30–33)

In the initial engagement, the Syrians lost about five thousand men, and Lysias, seeing the determination and courage of Judas's fighters, withdrew to Antioch to organize an even larger force.

Judas seized the opportunity to recapture Jerusalem. When the Maccabees entered the city, they found the temple severely damaged and the altar defiled. The gates were burned, the courts overgrown with weeds. Appalled, they tore their garments, wept, covered their heads with ashes, fell on their faces, and cried out to the God of heaven.

Judas ordered his troops to attack the garrison in the citadel while he selected priests to purify the temple. They removed the pagan idols, including the idolatrous altar, and ground the statue of Zeus to dust. They built an altar out of uncut stones, and the priests began offering daily sacrifices to the Lord. According to legend, the Maccabees found a cruse with only enough oil for one day, but miraculously the lamp burned for eight. The Jews celebrated the cleansing (164 BC) for eight days and decreed an annual commemoration that became known as the Feast of Hanukkah or "Festival of Lights."

While Antiochus was campaigning in Persia, a messenger reported that the Maccabees had defeated Lysias and his army, captured a large quantity of weapons, occupied Jerusalem, and destroyed "the abomination he had built on the altar" (1 Maccabees 6:7). Antiochus became overcome with grief and severe depression, certain his misfortunes were judgment for all the evil he had done in Jerusalem. He became ill and never recovered, eventually dying in 149 BC in Babylon, where Alexander the Great also had died.

Antiochus had designated his close friend Philip as successor, but Lysias placed Antiochus's young son (Antiochus V) on the throne and gave him the name Eupator. Furious when he heard the garrison in Jerusalem was under siege, Lysias quickly assembled another massive force including infantry, cavalry, and war elephants. He invaded Judea and defeated the Maccabees near Jerusalem.

Even so, Lysias suffered heavy casualties. Further, because Philip, whom Antiochus had appointed king, returned from Persia and was seeking to claim the empire by takeover, Lysias was forced to return to Antioch without total victory. The revolt was still alive, and the Jews controlled Jerusalem.

Lysias defeated Philip and took possession of the capital. However, Demetrius, a son of Seleucus, returned to Syria from Rome, and he became king when his supporters captured and killed both Antiochus V and Lysias.

Demetrius installed Alcimus as the new high priest in Jerusalem and sent a large force under the command of Bacchides, the Syrian governor. When the godless, treacherous Alcimus arrived, he assured the Hasidim he had come in peace; then, after he'd gained their confidence, he arrested and executed sixty of them. Bacchides returned to Syria, leaving behind a military unit for Alcimus to command.

Alcimus fought hard to hold on to the priesthood. He attempted a scorched-earth campaign throughout Judea to destroy the rebels, yet not only could he not best them, he couldn't even match them. When Judas reoccupied Jerusalem, Alcimus fled to Syria and proceeded to accuse Judas of atrocities.

Demetrius now ordered Nicanor, one of his best generals, to wipe out the Maccabees. Nicanor, who hated the Jews, decided on deception to capture Judas and proposed a peaceful meeting. Judas found out it was a trap and escaped; subsequently, in a battle against the Maccabees, Nicanor was killed, and his army withdrew. For a brief period the Jews enjoyed peace.

Ultimately, having lost Nicanor, Demetrius entrusted Bacchides and Alcimus with a gigantic force to crush the Hasidim. When Judas's men saw the size of the Syrian army, all but eight hundred deserted him. Many of the rest tried to persuade him to withdraw; Judas, expecting a miracle, attacked.

Judas Maccabeus was killed, and his remaining soldiers were scattered. Jonathan and Simon buried their brother in the family tomb at Modin.

All Israel mourned for the death of "the Hammerer." They cried out,
"How is our champion fallen,
The savior of Israel!" (1 Maccabees 9:21)

The death of Judas actually served to fuel the revolt. More and more zealous Jews joined the Maccabees, who chose to follow Jonathan. When Bacchides learned of Jonathan's appointment as leader, he personally led a force to kill him and thought he'd trapped him at the Jordan, but the Maccabees escaped across the river after killing about a thousand Syrians. The survivors did not pursue.

Bacchides returned to Jerusalem and took hostage the sons of leading citizens, but in the end he was unable to achieve victory; he gave up and returned to Syria. Jonathan, who turned out to be clever, sent envoys to negotiate peace and to attain the release of the Jewish hostages. Under the terms of their agreement, Bacchides never again invaded Judea.

Feeling that he found pervasive godlessness in Jerusalem, Jonathan initially set up his government in Michmash and gained a large following. Meanwhile, intrigue and internal struggles threatened Seleucid rule in Syria. Alexander Epiphanes claimed he was the son of Antiochus Epiphanes and challenged Demetrius for the throne.

Through this turn of events, in the ensuing conflict, both Alexander and Demetrius appealed to Jonathan for support. Demetrius granted him authority to raise an army and make weapons. Jonathan then aggressively returned to Jerusalem and placed his government there. Alexander, also negotiating, offered him the office of high priest and sent a purple robe and a gold crown.

Again, the descendants of Zadok had been high priests for centuries, and Jonathan wasn't in the priestly line. (Zadok was appointed by Solomon when he removed Abiathar, a descendant of Eli, from the position [1 Kings 2:27; 4:2]. Henceforth, Zadok's name itself was used to identify those in the line.) Nevertheless, Jonathan didn't hesitate to accept Alexander's bid and officiated as high priest for the Feast of Tabernacles in 152 BC.

Not to be outdone, Demetrius promised to exempt the Jews from taxes, to release Jewish prisoners, to give the high priest additional political power, and to pay for the temple's maintenance. This Jonathan and his supporters didn't accept—they thought it was a ploy and continued to support Alexander.

When Demetrius was killed in a battle against Alexander, his son returned to Syria and raised a large army. Demetrius II now challenged Jonathan either to fight or to bow the knee. Opting for the former, Jonathan defeated the Syrians at Azotus, and after Alexander heard of the victory he rewarded Jonathan with a royal seal of friendship and power.

Though the Jews preferred Alexander to Demetrius II, they had no real interest in supporting any Syrian ruler. They wanted independence, and before long an opportunity arose. Ptolemy VI of Egypt sent his army to Syria on the pretense of helping Alexander, then attacked instead. Alexander fled to Arabia, but rather than protect him, the Arab chieftain cut off his head and sent it to Ptolemy.

Jonathan felt he had an opening to declare independence. He laid siege to the Akra, the fortress that symbolized Syrian rule in Jerusalem. Yet before he could capture it, Demetrius II, now the king, summoned him to explain his actions. The Jews were not prepared for a military conflict with the Syrians, so Jonathan brought silver and gold and other gifts to the meeting. The king confirmed him as high priest and honored him as one of "the King's Friends." When Jonathan requested exemption from taxes, Demetrius II agreed and also placed three Samaritan provinces under his control.

Believing his rule had been secured, Demetrius II disbanded the army except for foreign mercenaries, causing a military revolt. Tryphon, a general and former supporter of Alexander, realized that the king lacked the army's support and staged a coup to overthrow him.

Then, though Antiochus VI was only a teenager, Tryphon declared *him* king. From Jonathan's perspective, Demetrius II had reneged on his promises of land and money (in exchange for support), so he sided with Antiochus. After they defeated Demetrius II, the young Antiochus, under Tryphon's guardianship, rewarded Jonathan with retention of the office of high priest and with additional territory. He too declared Jonathan a "King's Friend" and appointed his brother Simon governor of the Philistine coastal area.

On top of gaining control over more Judean territory, Jonathan also renewed the treaties Judas had made with Rome and Sparta. While the Roman senate declared Rome a "Friend of Judah," it had no intention of intervening in the struggle with the Seleucids.

But now Tryphon, who distrusted the Maccabees, invaded Judah with a large army. When Jonathan in turn met him with forty thousand strong, Tryphon, instead of engaging, tricked him, saying, "Why have you come with such a large force? Send them home. We have come in peace. Accompany me to Ptolemais (a Mediterranean seaport), and I will give it to you, and other cities as well."

The ruse worked. Jonathan took only an escort of a thousand with him. Once inside the city of Ptolemais, the Syrians locked the gates, slaughtered Jonathan's men, and took him prisoner.

Tryphon then sent his army into Galilee to wipe out the freedom fighters. When Jonathan's men heard of his capture, they vowed to fight to the death. And even though the Syrians had to withdraw, Tryphon made plans to re-invade Judea.

Free From "the Yoke of the Gentiles"

With the Seleucids poised to assault, the Jews, without their leader, panicked. But Simon, the last of the sons of Mattathias, assembled the leaders in Jerusalem and vowed to continue the struggle: "Heaven forbid that I should flee from danger. I will take up the cause of the nation and this holy place." Re-infused with courage, the people shouted, "You shall be our leader in place of Judas and your brother Jonathan!" (1 Maccabees 13:5–8). Simon quickly assembled an army and fortified Jerusalem. There would be no easy victory for the Syrians.

When Tryphon was confronted by Simon and his forces, he promised to release Jonathan in exchange for a ransom of money and children. Simon paid the ransom. And then, true to form, Tryphon executed Jonathan and withdrew to Syria. Simon buried his brother in their village and built a monument to his father and his brothers.

The Seleucid Empire, increasingly weak, had divided into two factions. One supported Demetrius II; the other was loyal to Antiochus VI, under Tryphon's charge. Tryphon, determined to seize power, murdered the young Antiochus VI, but unexpectedly this turned into disaster for Tryphon and opportunity for Simon.

When Tryphon lost popular support, Simon recognized Demetrius as king and sent a delegation requesting exemption from taxation. Needing the Jews' support, Demetrius granted them immunity, also recognizing Simon as high priest and a "King's Friend." Simon had chosen wisely; Israel was at last independent. First Maccabees records, at last, that "Israel was released from the Gentile yoke" (13:41).

Simon moved quickly to secure and solidify the new nation, extending Israel's territory and fortifying strategic cities. He captured the coastal towns of Gazara and Joppa (a port city). He captured the Akra, the final Syrian stronghold in Jerusalem, by starving its defenders.

All the areas that Gentiles had controlled were cleansed. The temple was rededicated to the Lord and furnished with sacred vessels. Newly minted coins bore the inscription "Holy Jerusalem" and "Shekel of Israel." During Simon's rule, the Jews enjoyed peace and prosperity.

Providence again seemed with the Maccabees. Demetrius marched east with his army to capture Tryphon, but after he entered Media, the king of the Medes and Persians defeated his army and imprisoned him. When Rome and Sparta heard Jonathan was dead and Simon was ruling as high priest, they sent a letter to Simon renewing their friendship to the Jews. Simon confirmed the alliance by gifting money and a large gold shield to the Romans.

The people saw what Simon had accomplished, and they wanted to show their gratitude to him and his brothers. In 140 BC they placed an inscription on Mount Zion honoring Simon for his patriotism and his success in establishing a free Jewish state. Part of it read, "The Jews and their priests confirmed Simon as their leader and high priest in perpetuity

Jesus and the Feast of Dedication

It was a cold December day in Jerusalem, when Jesus criticized the Jewish religious leaders for misleading Israel (John 10:1–21). God, the shepherd of his people (Psalm 23; Isaiah 40:10–11), had appointed religious and political leaders as shepherds to care for them (Isaiah 56:9–12; Jeremiah 23:1–4). To these leaders who'd become corrupt, Jesus said, "I am the good shepherd" (John 10:11). Instead of exploiting and abandoning the flock, he was willing to die to save them (John 10:14–18).

The occasion was the Feast of Dedication (John 10:22). Two hundred years before, Antiochus IV had profaned the temple by dedicating it to Zeus and sacrificing a pig on the altar, a sacrilege that ignited the Maccabean Revolt. About three years later, Judas Maccabeus and his freedom fighters drove the Syrians out of Jerusalem and rededicated the temple to the Lord. Judas was said to have found only enough oil for one day, but miraculously it burned for eight, and so the feast is also known as *Hanukkah* (Hebrew), or the Feast of Lights (originally called the Feast of the Maccabees).

At that time the priests used Ezekiel 34 to examine their service to God. Ezekiel draws a sharp contrast between Israel's false shepherds, who used their position for their own selfish interests instead of caring for the flock, and God, the "Good Shepherd" who will rescue and care for his sheep. By alluding to Ezekiel 34, Jesus implies (1) that he has come to fulfill the Lord's promises to faithfully shepherd his people and (2) that Israel's current leaders are corrupt and condemned.

until the true prophet should appear" (1 Maccabees 14:41). Plainly, messianic expectations were high, and some may have even thought Simon was Israel's long-awaited deliverer. Simon accepted the positions of both leader and high priest and was given absolute authority over all political and religious matters.

After the capture of Demetrius, his brother Antiochus VII (Sidetes) became king, with a first goal of capturing or killing Tryphon, who'd taken refuge in the city of Dor. Though twice surrounded and besieged, Tryphon still managed to escape.

Antiochus also sent a delegate to Jerusalem, demanding that the Jews pay tribute and surrender land he accused them of having taken from the Syrians. Simon refused and ordered his sons Judas and John (Hyrcanus) to organize and prepare the army.

When the Syrians invaded Judea, the Maccabees were ready. The decisive battle took place near Modin. Judas was wounded, but the Jews won in a rout. The Seleucid general barely escaped.

What their enemies accepted could not be accomplished by military victory, they again attempted to achieve by treachery. For example, the Egyptian governor Ptolemy plotted to take control of the Jewish state and turn it over to Antiochus Sidetes. He invited Simon and his sons to a party, then murdered the last of the Maccabees, and all but one son, while they were drunk. He sent assassins to kill the sole survivor, John Hyrcanus, but Hyrcanus discovered the scheme and had the assassins executed. He fortified Jerusalem and thus was ready for Ptolemy when he tried to occupy the city.

Simon's death marked the end of the Maccabean Period (when it is differentiated from the subsequent Hasmonean Period). The Jews were free, and Israel was an independent state. However, the old generation that had fought and died for freedom was passing. A new generation was in place to rule. (The name Hasmonean was given to the descendants of Simon in honor of Hasmon, an ancestor of Mattathias's sons.)

Jesus and Paul and the Maccabean Period

Whether or not Antiochus IV's ruthless attempt to eradicate Judaism would have succeeded without the revolt is uncertain, but his tyranny ignited Jewish fervency for the worship of the Lord and fueled nationalistic expectations for the promised messianic kingdom. Syrian oppression and later Roman occupation kept alive Israel's hope for the Messiah, so at the time of Christ many in Israel believed the time was near when God would intervene to rescue his people. Many, but not all, expected a military leader like David to overthrow their oppressors.

Messianic hope prompted Jesus' message known as the Olivet Discourse (Matthew 24–25). When leaving the temple, in response to his disciples' comment about its magnificence, Jesus foretold its total destruction, and they connected his prediction with his return as Israel's Messiah-King. He then explained to them what would happen in the future.

The outcome of the appointments first of Jonathan and then of Simon as high priest and ruler of the Jews was that the high priesthood became a hereditary position in possession of the Hasmoneans. Furthermore, what God had intended as a spiritual position became primarily political.

The result was the variable but increasing corruption of Israel's highest leader.

Though the high priests later referenced in the New Testament were not directly connected with the priesthood of the Hasmonean era, the office had remained political and hereditary. At the time of Jesus, Caiaphas (r. AD 13–36) was high priest. His father-in-law, Annas, had held the office previously, yet though the Romans had removed him, the Jews still referred to him as the high priest (Luke 3:2; Acts 4:6), probably because they believed the office was an appointment for life.

After Jesus raised Lazarus, his popularity skyrocketed (John 11:45). As the Sanhedrin became aware of the rising tide of support, they feared an uprising against Roman rule, a national disaster. Caiaphas recommended that it would be better to kill Jesus than risk reprisals. John interpreted his counsel as a prophecy about Jesus' sacrificial death (vv. 45–52).

After Jesus' arrest, the soldiers took him first to Annas for questioning. Unable to get Jesus to incriminate himself, Annas sent him to the official high priest, his son-in-law Caiaphas, for trial before the Sanhedrin (18:19–24). Caiaphas concluded Jesus had committed blasphemy by claiming that as the Son of Man he had divine authority to judge them (Mark 14:60–64). He then sent Jesus to Pilate, which resulted in a Roman trial and crucifixion.

Both Annas and Caiaphas questioned Peter and John about the healing of the lame man and their preaching about Christ's resurrection (Acts 4:5–7).

When Paul was arrested in Jerusalem, he was brought before the high priest Ananias (r. AD 47–58). When he ordered a guard to slap Paul, Paul called Ananias a "whitewashed wall," a stinging insult that was an accusation of hypocrisy (23:1–5). In other words, Ananias looked clean and sturdy on the outside but was filthy and decaying on the inside; Paul apparently apologized by quoting Exodus 22:28, which commands respect for rulers.

Paul's statement then that he did not know the high priest is somewhat puzzling, and there's no explanation in the text. It's my opinion that his comment may have been sarcasm. To paraphrase, he may have meant something like, "I didn't know a man such as this could be high priest," since Ananias was notoriously corrupt. For instance, according to Josephus, he stole the tithes that belonged to the priests (*Ant.* 20.9.2).

Questions for Discussion

1. In Romans 13:1–7, Paul says believers are to submit to governing authorities. Regarding the pre-Christian Maccabees, do you believe the revolt against the Syrians was justified? Discuss how Christians should respond to unjust rulers.

2. At the Feast of Dedication (Hanukkah), the priests used Ezekiel 34 to examine their ministry as the people's shepherds. Read John 10:1–30 and discuss (a) the origin of the Feast of Dedication and (b) the implications of Jesus' claim to be the Good Shepherd in contrast to Israel's leaders.

3. Discuss how Syrian (Seleucid) policies and tactics inflamed Jewish hopes for a messianic deliverer. What were the majority and minority expectations for a Messiah at the time of Christ? What are the majority expectations of American Christians today—or does the majority even have expectations?

4. We don't have the whole picture, by any means, but how much do you think divine providence (versus courage and strategizing) was responsible for the Maccabees' victories over superior forces? Discuss your answer.

5. Discuss the advantages and disadvantages of combining the position of political/military leader with the office of high priest during the Maccabean Period. To what extent should religious leaders today be involved in politics?

4

A House Divided
Against Itself Cannot Stand

The Hasmonean Period

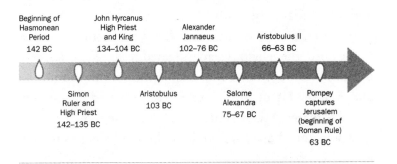

Introduction

(AD 29: It was the third year of Jesus' ministry, and the last week before his crucifixion. He was in Jerusalem when he denounced the Jewish leaders.)

Jesus was furious. Turning to the crowds and his disciples, he said, "The scribes and Pharisees love their prestige, but

(Source: Josephus, *Antiquities* 13.8–14.7)

the truth is they're hypocrites and blind fools. They do not practice what they teach" (see Matthew 23).

He'd had it with the religious leaders. He called them whitewashed tombs, attractive on the outside yet defiled on the inside. Obsessed with outward ritual purity, they totally ignored matters of the heart. Instead of leading people to God, he charged, they were leading them to hell.

Though the religious leaders had opposed Jesus from the beginning of his ministry for ignoring their traditions, the conflict exploded during what became known as Passion Week. On Sunday, he had come into Jerusalem on a donkey in fulfillment of Zechariah's prophecy about Israel's Messiah-King. The people honored him by throwing palm branches and their robes in his path.

However, in contrast to the people, who were singing praises to the Lord, the religious leaders feared Jesus. They *despised* one another, yet nonetheless the Pharisees, the Sadducees, and even the Herodians joined forces to get rid of him. On Tuesday, many of them confronted him, asking embarrassing questions they hoped would discredit him by exposing him as a false prophet.

What led to his scathing denunciations? What had happened to Israel's leaders that caused Jesus to harshly condemn them? Who *were* the Pharisees, Sadducees, and Herodians (none of whom are mentioned in the Old Testament)? Why were they so corrupt? Why were they unwilling to accept Jesus as their promised Messiah, and why did they want to get rid of him?

The answer to these questions is found in the Hasmonean Period of Israel's history (142/135–63 BC), an era characterized generally by political intrigue and religious corruption. After the death of Simon, the last son of Mattathias, the state was led by rulers who were mostly weak, mostly ineffective, and more concerned about personal wealth and power than the nation's future and the people's spiritual life.

John Hyrcanus: "Friend of the Sadducees"

"I cannot believe it. I will not stand for this. The man is not qualified," Eleazar, a leader of the Pharisees, complained to his wife.

"But why are you so angry?" she asked.

"There is a rumor that the mother of Hyrcanus was a prisoner of the Greeks," he answered. "Only a *pure* Jew can serve as high priest. What were the circumstances of his conception? The man may be only *part* Jewish. You know our law."

"What can be done?"

"I will confront him. I will demand that he step down."

John Hyrcanus (r. 135–104 BC), the most capable of the Hasmonean rulers, faced a major threat early on when Antiochus VII (Sidetes) invaded Judea and surrounded Jerusalem. After a year of siege, Hyrcanus surrendered the city to the Seleucids, who destroyed the defensive walls before withdrawing. The Jews did not lose their independence completely but once again became subject to Syrian rule. Hyrcanus had to relinquish control of the coastal cities the Maccabees had annexed and also send tribute and hostages.

It seemed that providence, though, was aiding the Jews. When Hyrcanus provided supplies for Antiochus and joined him in a campaign against the Parthians (a political kingdom previously a part of the ancient Persian Empire. At the height of its might, the Parthian Empire stretched from modern-day Turkey to modern-day eastern Iran), Antiochus chose to attack on a day holy to the Jews, and thus Hyrcanus and his forces did not march with the Syrians. The Parthians killed Antiochus and destroyed a sizeable part of his army.

When Hyrcanus heard of the defeat and death of Antiochus, he seized the opportunity to strengthen the Jewish nation. He extended territorial boundaries in all directions and captured several coastal cities on the trade routes between Egypt in the south and Syria in the north. Control of these cities provided a major source of income. He also conquered and annexed Idumea (ancient Edom, to the southeast of Israel) and forced the Idumeans to convert to Judaism by undergoing circumcision.

Hyrcanus knew the value of alliances with powerful nations. He sent a delegation to Rome to renew "a league of friendship" as the Romans were expanding their empire through military conquest. The delegation asked the Senate to return land Antiochus had taken, to compensate them for the destruction of their land, and to give them letters for safe return to Israel. The Romans agreed and recognized the Jews as "a friendly people" (*Ant.* 13.9.2).

Hyrcanus likewise was a capable military leader. He fueled the ancient hostility between Jews and Samaritans by invading Samaria and, after a year-long siege, capturing Shechem, the capital, and destroying the Samaritan temple on Mount Gerazim. Still not satisfied, Hyrcanus ravaged the city and then flooded it in an effort to remove any evidence that it ever existed.

We noted in chapter 3 that Jews who fanatically resisted Hellenism were known as the Hasidim. The Pharisees, first mentioned during the time of John Hyrcanus, carried forward Hasidic beliefs and lifestyle in all their strictness. Because of their loyalty to Jewish traditions, the Pharisees became the party of the people and Israel's most powerful religious party. In contrast, Jews who adopted and advocated the Greek way of life became known as the Sadducees. Though not as numerous as the Pharisees, they became a potent political and religious party with dominant control over the temple and the temple ritual.

Hyrcanus was not as diplomatic in religious matters as he was in political affairs. Though initially he had a good relationship with the Pharisees, this changed after a group of them attended a gathering by his invitation. When asked what they thought of his leadership, most heaped on praise, even commending him as a man of virtue. One, however, had a different opinion.

Eleazar confronted Hyrcanus over the issue of his mother, whom Eleazar said had been held captive by the Greeks. If Hyrcanus were an illegitimate son, he would be disqualified from serving as high priest. Since he could not prove otherwise, Eleazar said, he should give up the position and serve only as Israel's civil governor.

Insulted, Hyrcanus demanded that the Pharisees punish Eleazar. They agreed to flog but not execute him. Hyrcanus, further infuriated, left the Pharisee party, joined the Sadducees, and abolished the laws the Pharisees had imposed on the people.

Josephus explains the implications of this action. Again, the Pharisees, the party of the people, were loyal to the traditions of Judaism. The Sadducees, the party of the wealthy, disagreed with the Pharisees about which traditions the Law of Moses required. By aligning himself with the Sadducees, Hyrcanus distanced himself from the common people (*Ant.* 13.10.6).

A Comparison of Pharisees and Sadducees

Pharisees	Sadducees
The nucleus of the religious and academic leadership.	The nucleus of the priestly, political, and social aristocracy.
Taught that the soul is immortal, there is a future bodily resurrection, there is future reward or punishment.	Taught that there is no resurrection, no reward or punishment.
Believed in the existence of angels and spirits, good and bad.	Claimed there are neither angels nor spirits.
Predestinarians, yet said that man has a free will and is morally responsible.	Emphasized the absolute freedom of the human will.
Held tradition and the written Law to be joint rules of faith and practice.	Maintained that the Old Testament was the only infallible rule of faith and practice.
Magnified traditional Judaism and made it the basis of a vast system of minute laws to regulate Hellenism.	Broke away from traditional Judaism and placed it side by side with (if not beneath) contemporary life in Israel.
Sought to gain salvation by good works, which externalized their whole religious life.	Lived for this life only.
Activities confined mostly to synagogue.	Activities confined mostly to temple.

Aristobulus: "A Lover of the Greeks"

When John Hyrcanus died (104 BC), his arrogant and ambitious oldest son, apparently against what his father had wished, rose to the throne. The first act of Aristobulus, who had such a strong passion for the Greek way of life that he was called "a lover of the Greeks" (*Ant*. 13.11.3), was to declare himself the ruler. By any measure, his rule was a disaster for the nation. Aristobulus was insanely suspicious of potential rivals, including those within his own family. He trusted one brother, Antigonus, but had the others incarcerated. After imprisoning his mother, he ordered her starved to death.

Not surprisingly, the real enemies of Aristobulus used his paranoia to their advantage, secretly informing him that his one favored brother planned to steal the throne. Then when he became ill, he ordered his guards to kill Antigonus if he visited while armed. Totally unaware he was in any danger, Antigonus came one day to show Aristobulus his new suit of armor and never even saw the king, whose guards quickly murdered him.

Aristobulus never recovered his health and ruled only one year. While grieving for Antigonus, he died of some painful and bloody intestinal disease, which he thought was divine judgment for his crimes against his family.

Alexander Jannaeus: "The Treacherous King From Galilee"

When Aristobulus died, his wife released his remaining brothers and made Jannaeus king. Previous Hasmonean leaders had *ruled* like kings, yet Jannaeus, who also ruled as high priest, was the first to take the actual title of "King." Further, he took the surname *Alexander,* after Alexander the Great.

Jannaeus (r. 103–76 BC) had been raised in Galilee. His father, John Hyrcanus, hated him so much he never permitted him to be in his presence. When he believed God had appeared to him in a dream to say that Jannaeus would be his successor, he banished Jannaeus (back to Galilee) to prevent it.

Jannaeus would attempt to capture Ptolemais for an additional seaport on the Mediterranean but have to withdraw when Ptolemy IX (Lathyrus) arrived from Cyprus with a large army to rescue the city. Now, Ptolemy had been driven out of Egypt by Cleopatra III, its queen; Alexander had convinced him to form an alliance and invade. However, he had then underhandedly informed Cleopatra of *Ptolemy's* invasion plan.

In retaliation, Ptolemy invaded *Judea* and wrought terrible slaughter. He ordered his soldiers to boil and eat women and children as sacrifices. Survivors of the carnage thought Ptolemy's soldiers were cannibals.

On the domestic front, Jannaeus despised the Pharisees, and he showed contempt for their beliefs at the Feast of Tabernacles by pouring sacred water on his feet instead of on the altar. Spectators, horrified, threw at him the tree branches they were carrying to observe the feast. When he commanded his men to restore order, they attacked and killed six thousand defenseless Jews.

His brutality combined with rumors of immorality and flouting of sacred traditions convinced the Pharisees he had to be overthrown. They revolted by forming a strange alliance: They asked King Demetrius of Syria to help them, and thus Jewish supporters of the Pharisees were allied with Greeks against their Hasmonean king.

Jannaeus strengthened his own army (of Jewish soldiers) by hiring Greek mercenaries. Before the first battle, he tried to persuade opposing Jews to desert the Syrian force; Demetrius encouraged Alexander's mercenaries to join his army. Neither was successful. After a fierce battle, a defeated Alexander fled into the Judean hills. The Syrians would have won a complete victory, but six thousand Pharisees decided the Syrians were a greater threat than Alexander, and when they switched sides, Demetrius withdrew to Syria.

Thereafter the cruel and unforgiving Alexander Jannaeus went on a rampage of revenge against the Jews who had rebelled. His soldiers captured eight hundred of the Pharisee leaders and brought them to Jerusalem; then he invited his Sadducee supporters to a banquet and had the captives crucified for entertainment. When the men were nailed to crosses, he had their wives and children brought before them and had his soldiers slit their throats while the men watched, helpless and in agony.

Jannaeus died from an alcohol-related illness. Though motivated by political expediency, on his deathbed he advised his wife to give control of the kingdom to the Pharisees in exchange for their political support. He hoped they'd give him an honorable funeral rather than abuse his body.

Alexandra: "A Repentant Queen"

Salome Alexandra (r. 76–67 BC) was almost seventy. She followed her husband's counsel and made peace with the Pharisees. She convinced them he'd been a good king, somehow, and despite his incredible treachery and brutality they actually grieved over his death and honored him at his funeral.

Because Alexandra seemed genuinely sorry for Alexander's crimes, the people supported her. Even so, because she was a woman she could not serve as high priest. She appointed her oldest son, Hyrcanus, to the office and placed her other son, Aristobulus, in charge of the military.

Though she retained the title of *Queen,* she also gave the Pharisees extensive control over religious and political affairs. They used this power to restore the traditions Jannaeus had abolished, and they demanded the punishment of those who had murdered their eight hundred leaders. They themselves killed several Sadducees before Aristobulus intervened and convinced Alexandra to stop the violence.

Except for such inter-party fighting, the nation was mostly at peace during her rule. Aristobulus unsuccessfully tried to capture Damascus, and Alexandra bribed the king of Armenia to keep him from invading Judea. Afraid the Pharisees would seize power when his mother died, Aristobulus secretly built support and managed to organize his own army.

Alexandra reigned nine years. When she died, her two sons engaged in their own power struggle.

Hyrcanus II and Aristobulus II: "Sibling Rivals"

Though Alexandra had appointed Hyrcanus II to succeed her, he wasn't interested in ruling the nation and quickly surrendered both the throne and the priesthood when Aristobulus II threatened Jerusalem with a large army of Sadducees. Hyrcanus negotiated a pact of friendship with Aristobulus, and the former's daughter married the latter's oldest son.

While Hyrcanus had yielded power to Aristobulus, however, this sibling rivalry had by no means been quelled. Herod Antipater, governor of Idumea and a friend of Hyrcanus, was a troublemaker and opportunist. Plotting to intervene in the politics of the Jewish state, he persuaded Hyrcanus that his brother intended to kill him. Then he made an arrangement with King Aretas III of Nabatea to give Hyrcanus refuge in the city of Petra. Hyrcanus promised to return to Aretas twelve cities that Alexander Jannaeus had taken if he would help him overthrow Aristobulus.

With his Nabatean allies, Hyrcanus invaded Judea and easily defeated the forces of Aristobulus, who fled to Jerusalem and barricaded himself in the temple complex. Only the Sadducean priests inside with him continued to support him. The people favored Hyrcanus.

Now, the temple complex was a formidable fortress; even the combined force of Jews and Arabians could not break through the defenses. The attackers decided to seek divine help and ordered a righteous priest named Onias to curse Aristobulus and his supporters. Instead, Onias prayed for the Jews on *both* sides of the conflict and was stoned to death.

When Passover came, Aristobulus and the priests requested animals for the traditional sacrifices. They were told they'd have to pay for what they wanted, yet after they gave the money, the animals weren't delivered. When they realized they'd been cheated, the priests asked God to avenge them, and a violent storm destroyed crops in Judea.

Aristobulus escaped when he bribed Pompey's general, who ordered Aretas to lift the siege.

Pompey and the Romans

While the two brothers were locked in a standoff, other winds were blowing—and events were occurring—that would profoundly alter the fate of the nation. The Roman general Pompey was sent to protect the empire's interests in the

East, and while in Armenia he dispatched one of his officers, Scaurus, to Syria. After both Hyrcanus and Aristobulus sent delegations with money and promises in exchange for Roman support, Scaurus determined that Aristobulus was the more capable and reliable ally and ordered the Nabateans to withdraw from Judea. They did.

Aristobulus, suddenly back in power, craved revenge. He organized a large army, and then he pursued Hyrcanus and Aretas. His forces inflicted heavy casualties on the Nabateans and killed Herod Antipater's brother.

When Pompey himself arrived in Syria, it seemed everyone was anxious to make a treaty with Rome. Syrian, Egyptian, and Judean ambassadors poured on gifts and pledged their own support. After a brief campaign there in Syria, Pompey made Damascus his headquarters.

When Hyrcanus and Aristobulus reached Damascus to plead their cases, each complained that the other had deprived him of his right to rule. A third delegation wanted Pompey to remove both men from the office of high priest. Pompey ordered the brothers to cease all hostilities and promised he would make a decision after he had dealt with the Nabateans.

Aristobulus decided that Pompey would probably favor his brother, so he returned and began fortifying Jerusalem. When Pompey found out he was preparing for war, he marched on Jerusalem instead of Nabatea. He tried, unsuccessfully, to negotiate with Aristobulus, and then put the city under siege.

Some residents wanted to surrender to Pompey, but supporters of Aristobulus barricaded themselves inside the temple complex. Before long the Romans, like others before them, realized the Jews would not fight on the Sabbath, so every week on that day they built earthen ramps to move their battering rams into position. On the Day of Atonement in 63 BC, after a three-month siege, they broke through. Twelve thousand defenders either were killed or committed suicide by jumping from the walls (some also by setting their homes on fire). The soldiers mercilessly slaughtered the priests, who refused to fight or even flee. Pompey desecrated the temple by entering the Holy of Holies with his officers, but he had sufficient respect for Judaism that he did not allow his soldiers to plunder the temple.

Meanwhile, Hyrcanus had made a shrewd choice. He supported Pompey in the attack on Aristobulus by discouraging Jews from helping him during the siege. Pompey rewarded Hyrcanus with the office of high priest; in addition he gave him control of Jerusalem and five other districts.

The capture of Jerusalem and the occupation of the Jewish state was a major feat. In defeating another nation and adding territory, Pompey had earned the honor of a Roman triumph. He took Aristobulus, along with his sons and daughters, and other Jewish prisoners to Rome for his victory parade.

On the way to Rome, Alexander, the youngest of the sons, escaped and returned to Judea. He recruited a small army to overthrow his uncle, Hyrcanus, but didn't stand a chance against the Romans. Alexander wisely surrendered, and the Roman general spared his life.

The Jewish state had survived only eighty years. Josephus attributed the loss of independence, which the Maccabees had fought so courageously and fiercely to gain, to the seditious conflict between Aristobulus and Hyrcanus (*Ant.* 3.14.5). Even so, it's unlikely that even a unified Jewish state could have withstood the eastward expansion of the powerful Roman Empire.

Discussion Questions

1. Discuss (a) three or more differences between Pharisees and Sadducees and (b) three or more differences between denominations or churches in America now.

2. Discuss why John Hyrcanus, initially a friend of the Pharisees, became a bitter enemy and a Sadducee. Do you think a person's religious affiliation is important to their political career? Why or why not?

3. Regarding the Romans taking advantage of Jewish convictions to conquer Jerusalem, do you think the Jews were foolish for refusing to fight on the Sabbath? Why or why not?

4. As to Jesus' denunciation of Jewish leaders, discuss what you believe he would find (a) commendable and (b) objectionable about Christian leaders today.

5

Herod the Great: "The Client King"

The Roman Period: Part I

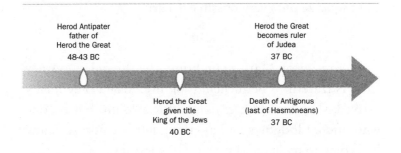

Herod Antipater
father of
Herod the Great
48-43 BC

Herod the Great
becomes ruler
of Judea
37 BC

Herod the Great
given title
King of the Jews
40 BC

Death of Antigonus
(last of Hasmoneans)
37 BC

Introduction

(5 BC: Palestine [Israel], conquered in 63 BC, is a Roman province.)

Like all empires, of all epochs, Rome needed money. So Emperor Augustus issued this decree: "I, Caesar, the Exalted One, order a census. Let it be known that every person in the

(Source: Josephus, *Antiquities* 14.8–16.11)

empire must register in the town of their birth." The order then was sent out immediately to all provinces.

Joseph the carpenter was working in his shop when the news reached him. "Augh! Those *Romans*," he muttered. "All they want is money. Taxes, taxes, more and more taxes—when will it stop?"

In the evening, back at home, Joseph told his wife.

"But the child is due at any time, Joseph," Mary said. "I want to give birth at home. *Must* it be Bethlehem? Cannot something be done?"

"There is nothing," he replied, sounding tired, resigned. "We have no choice. The Romans rule; the Romans require everyone to register. If they don't keep up-to-date rolls, they can't squeeze out every possible denarius."

As a result of Mary's condition, the three-day journey from Nazareth to Bethlehem took five. When they finally arrived, they looked everywhere for a room, but no one who offered lodgings had anything left because so many had come to register. Mary gave birth to Jesus, God's Son, in Bethlehem, exactly as Micah the prophet had foretold (Micah 5:2).

Israel was subject to Rome, but God, still in control, was providentially guiding history to fulfill his plan to save people from their sins.

To recap briefly from chapter 4: After he captured Jerusalem, Pompey placed Judea under Syria's military governor. He appointed Hyrcanus II high priest with political control over five Judean districts, then took Aristobulus and other captives to Rome to display them in his triumph.

On the way, Aristobulus's son Alexander somehow escaped, returned to Judea, and organized an army to overthrow Hyrcanus. He might've succeeded if the military governor hadn't sent soldiers to put down the rebellion. In the battle for Jerusalem, six thousand of his number were killed and captured. Alexander escaped and took refuge in a fortress north of Jericho, but when the Romans surrounded it, he surrendered in exchange for his life.

Because of Hyrcanus II's incompetence as an administrator, the Romans stripped him of political power while allowing him to retain his position as high priest. In some respects this was a positive development, as for the first time in decades the high priest was only a religious leader (and not a political ruler). However, from Idumea, Herod Antipater, a friend of Hyrcanus, was watching developments in Judea with keen interest.

Herod Antipater

Herod Antipater, governor of Idumea (Old Testament Edom, southeast of Israel), was a shrewd opportunist. With the removal of Hyrcanus from his position as governor, Antipater saw a chance to extend his power into Judea.

Antipater knew he needed Rome's support to extend his reach into Judea, so he was alert for an opportunity to win Roman favor. When General Gabinus launched a campaign to invade Egypt, he ran short on supplies. Antipater came to the rescue with food, weapons, and money.

Meanwhile, though Alexander had surrendered, he still was not willing to accept Roman rule and yield the high

Edom

The Herodian dynasty began with Herod Antipater. He and his family line became surrogate governors of the Jews under the Roman occupation of Israel but were never accepted as legitimate rulers because they were descendants of Esau, Jacob's despised brother.

The hostility between the Israelites and the Edomites began at birth, between Esau and Jacob, the twin sons of Isaac and Rebekah (Genesis 25:19–34; 27:1–29; 33:1–17). Because of his skin's reddish color and his thick hair even at birth, his parents named the firstborn *Esau*; they named the other *Jacob* because he was born grasping his brother's heel. ("Jacob" sounds like the Hebrew for "heel" or "deceiver.") Esau eventually settled in an area with reddish soil southeast of the Dead Sea. "Edom," which sounds like the Hebrew word ('*admoni*) for "red," also is known as Seir (which means "hairy").

Jacob manipulated his brother to give up his birthright for a bowl of tasty stew and later tricked his aged father into giving him the patriarchal blessing usually granted to the firstborn. Esau was so angry he wanted to kill his brother; Jacob fled, and the brothers were apart for twenty years (Genesis 25–28; 35–36).

Even though the two of them then reconciled, the hostility persisted to the time of David (2 Samuel 8:11–15) and Amaziah, who conquered the Edomites (2 Kings 14:7; 2 Chronicles 25:11–12). After they gained their independence more than two centuries later (735 BC), they remained hereditary enemies of the Jews.

priesthood to Hyrcanus. While Gabinus and the Roman army were in Egypt, he organized a revolt against Hyrcanus; news reached Gabinus, who returned to Judea and engaged Alexander's forces near Mount Tabor. The Romans killed ten thousand Jews. Alexander escaped but was later captured and beheaded by one of Pompey's generals.

The political situation in Rome itself was destabilized when powerful individuals began maneuvering for control of the empire. When Julius Caesar seized power, Pompey and the senate fled. Caesar, needing an ally in the East, released Aristobulus from prison, planning to send him back to Judea in command of two Roman legions. Aristobulus, though, never made it. He was poisoned by supporters of Pompey before he could even leave Rome.

Meanwhile, both Antipater and Hyrcanus benefitted from their support of the Romans. When Caesar launched another campaign against Egypt, Antipater, with the help of Hyrcanus, proved himself a useful ally in recruiting an auxiliary army of Jews, Syrians, and Arabians and also persuading Jews living in Egypt to fight on his side. He then saved his army from costly defeat by personally leading a counterattack when it appeared the Egyptians would overrun his right flank. When Caesar received the report of this courage, he placed Antipater in charge of some of the most difficult battles in Egypt, granted him Roman citizenship, and exempted him from paying taxes in the territories under his control.

Antipater also demonstrated his diplomatic skill when another son of Aristobulus appealed to Caesar for restoration to power in Judea. Antigonus charged that Antipater and Hyrcanus were responsible for the death of his father and brother and accused them of using violence to govern Judea. Having received from Caesar the opportunity to respond, Antipater denied the accusations and reminded Caesar of how he'd helped him in the war against Egypt. He said Aristobulus and Alexander were enemies of Rome and had deserved their punishment.

The defense was effective. Caesar made Antipater procurator (governor) of Judea, confirmed Hyrcanus as high priest, and granted the Jews religious freedom and clearance to rebuild the Jerusalem walls Pompey had destroyed.

Antipater moved quickly to consolidate his power in Judea. He rebuilt the walls of Jerusalem and convinced the Jews that it was in their best interest to accept him as their governor and Hyrcanus as king. He argued it was better to have them as gentle rulers than tyrants and the Romans as their enemies.

Antipater then decided that Hyrcanus was *not* adequately competent, so he made his son Phasael governor of Jerusalem and its surrounding districts. Further, he appointed as governor of Galilee his second son, Herod.

This Herod, brilliant, shrewd, driven, and ruthless, would become "Herod the Great."

Origins of Herod the Great

Though he was young when he became Galilee's governor (probably not fifteen, as stated by Josephus), he was ambitious and aggressive. He won the respect of Syria's governor by eliminating outlaw bands that harassed and robbed Syrians living in his district. He was able to capture and execute

Hezekiah, a renowned leader of one such band, and most of his followers. While the Syrians were grateful to Herod for providing peace and safety, his actions, which blatantly disregarded Jewish law, offended the Jews.

Furthermore, Antipater's increasing power in Judea alarmed the Jewish leadership, who considered Antipater and his sons dangerous and cruel tyrants. "How long will you allow this man and his sons to exploit our nation? Don't you see that he and his sons are actually ruling Judea? You have only been given the title of king but have no power" (*Ant.* 14.9.3). They also reminded him that Jewish law prohibited anyone from imposing the death penalty without a decision of the Sanhedrin in Jerusalem. Herod had completely ignored this in executing Hezekiah and his men.

After some of the mothers of the dead likewise protested, Hyrcanus summoned Herod to Jerusalem. On his father's advice, Herod came, dressed in a purple robe and accompanied by imposing guards. The governor of Syria already had warned Hyrcanus against punishing Herod; in addition, not only was the Sanhedrin intimidated, but only one member had the courage to confront.

Simeon stood and said,

I have never witnessed such arrogance. When men are summoned to appear before the Sanhedrin on charges of murder, they are usually submissive and fearful. But Herod has come here dressed like a king and with an armed escort. He dares us to condemn him. However, my complaint is not so much against Herod as it is against you. Listen carefully, "Our God is great," if you acquit Herod of these charges, he will one day take vengeance on you and Hyrcanus. (*Ant.* 14.9.4)

(Simeon would later be proven right: When Herod became king, he executed Hyrcanus and the entire Sanhedrin except for Simeon, whom he considered courageous and just.)

When Hyrcanus realized the high court intended to impose the death penalty on Herod, he dismissed the Sanhedrin and advised him to leave Jerusalem. Herod returned to Damascus, but not for long—he was determined to get revenge on the Jews. He bribed Syria's governor for the position of general of the army and returned, intent on attacking. Antipater and Phasael persuaded him not to assault the city, saying he couldn't be certain of victory and reminding him that Hyrcanus was a Herodian, one of his supporters. Herod called off the attack, satisfied that he'd terrified the Jews with a massive show of strength.

While Caesar was in Rome preparing for a campaign in Egypt, Hyrcanus sent a delegation to renew the pact of friendship between the Jews and Romans. Caesar made a brass pillar and had engraved on it his decree that granted Roman citizenship to the Jews in Alexandria, confirmed Hyrcanus and his sons as perpetual high priest and priests, permitted the Jews to keep part of their tribute, and allowed them to worship according to their traditions. The decree read in part, "I will that Hyrcanus, the son of Alexander, and his children, be ethnarchs [subordinate local rulers] of the Jews forever, according to the customs of their forefathers, and that he and his sons be our confederates. . . . I permit these Jews to gather themselves together, according to the customs and laws of their forefathers, and to persist therein" (*Ant.* 14.10.2). The Jews were also granted control of Jerusalem and permission to strengthen its walls.

Herod's Path to Power

While Herod benefitted from Rome's political instability, most of the Jews were unfortunate victims. When Bassus, one of Pompey's supporters, assassinated Sextus Caesar, governor of Syria, war broke out between Bassus and the supporters of Caesar. Antipater joined forces with Caesar's generals.

As the conflict dragged on, Rome decided to intervene, but the political situation there shifted dramatically when Cassius and Brutus murdered Julius Caesar. Cassius invaded Syria and Judea, then imposed military rule on Judea and demanded higher taxes from its towns. Antipater, ever shrewd, appointed his sons to collect the taxes that the Romans demanded. Herod impressed them and cultivated their friendship with his ability for collecting taxes in Galilee. Cities that refused to pay were attacked, their citizens sold as slaves.

Thinking that Antipater's death would preserve the rule of Hyrcanus, Malichus, a zealous Jew, paid a servant to poison him at a dinner party. Both Herod and Phasael suspected Malichus had murdered their father, though he denied any involvement. When Herod reported to Cassius that his father had been murdered and that Malichus was responsible, Cassius gave permission for Herod to avenge his father's death. Using similar treachery, Herod invited Malichus to a party and ordered a group of officers to kill him. The assassins ambushed him and stabbed him to death as he approached the city of Tyre.

Julius Caesar's death left a power vacuum in Rome that Mark Anthony, one of his powerful generals, hoped to fill. But he faced the opposition of Cassius, one of Caesar's assassins and the army's general in the East. When Cassius withdrew his legions from Syria for the fight, Antigonus, son of Aristobulus, the last of the Hasmoneans, recruited an army and attempted to invade Judea. Herod engaged his forces as soon as they crossed the border and drove them out. When Herod returned to Jerusalem, Hyrcanus and the people honored him for his victory. Hyrcanus even agreed to let his granddaughter become Herod's second wife.

Because Anthony's troop strength had been depleted in the war he fought against Cassius, he withdrew to Syria to rebuild his army. In Tyre, a delegation of Jews complained to him about Herod's rule. Hyrcanus, when asked, defended Herod, who (with Phasael) gave Anthony a large sum of money—a bribe that proved more persuasive than the Jews. Anthony reconfirmed Herod and Phasael as tetrarchs (a position subordinate to ethnarch, or governor) and allowed Hyrcanus to remain as high priest. When the Jewish delegation protested the decision, Anthony's officers attacked them with daggers, killing some and wounding others. The rest fled.

Like numerous men, Mark Anthony came under the spell of Cleopatra VII, and the two became lovers. An affair with the Queen of Egypt had political benefits, but while Anthony was preoccupied with her in Alexandria, the Parthians invaded Syria.

Antigonus made an alliance with the invaders, promising them money and women if they would kill Herod and strip Hyrcanus of power. With the support of a detachment of Parthian cavalry, Antigonus infiltrated Jerusalem, yet was unable to defeat Herod even after a lengthy struggle. Then the Parthian general came to Jerusalem and proposed a meeting.

Phasael and Hyrcanus met with the Parthians; a suspicious Herod refused to attend, and his instincts were right. After entertaining Phasael and Hyrcanus, the Parthians seized them.

When Herod was informed they'd been taken captive and that the Parthians intended to kill him, he fled Jerusalem with his family, their servants, and a small unit of soldiers. He planned to take refuge in the fortress of Masada, but the size of his entourage compelled him instead to go to Idumea. The pursuant Parthians were repulsed in hand-to-hand combat.

Phasael and Hyrcanus were less fortunate. Because the Law prohibited anyone physically deformed from serving as high priest, Antigonus had Hyrcanus's ears cut off to prevent the Jews from reinstalling him. Phasael, meanwhile, considered death at enemy hands dishonorable, and because his hands were bound he bashed his head on a rock. He apparently did not die immediately but was poisoned by a woman sent to treat his wounds. Before he expired, he found out Herod had escaped, so he died with the satisfaction of knowing his brother would avenge his death.

Herod appealed to the king of Arabia for help, offering money and Phasael's seven-year-old son as a hostage, but the king refused for fear of the Parthians, who'd threatened retaliation on anyone who helped him. So Herod decided his best chance for survival was in Rome. He escaped to Egypt, and though Cleopatra invited him to stay, he made arrangements to sail on.

The journey was dangerous. The ship was destroyed in a violent storm, but after building another, Herod made it. In Rome, he told Mark Anthony how he'd barely escaped the Parthians, who'd invaded Judea, killed his brother, captured

Hyrcanus, and installed Antigonus as king. He said Anthony was his only hope—he'd risked everything to come.

Anthony was sympathetic. He considered Herod a loyal ally. He also hated Antigonus, whom he believed was an enemy of Rome, and Octavian Caesar, whom Antipater had helped in Egypt, agreed.

The senate was convened. Anthony informed them of the Parthian invasion of Judea and the installation of Antigonus as king. The Senate declared Antigonus to be Rome's enemy and surprised Herod by giving *him* the title of king. Having come to Rome as a fugitive, he left the Senate escorted by Anthony and Octavian as "King of the Jews."

Herod the "King"

Herod had the title; nonetheless, he was without a kingdom. He was in Rome, a thousand miles from Judea. The Parthians occupied his domain, and his brother and his family were now under siege in Masada.

His fortunes changed when the Senate ordered legions to drive the Parthians out of Syria. When they retreated south into Judea, the Romans pursued and camped near Jerusalem. The presence of the legions intimidated Antigonus, who bribed their general; the Romans withdrew, leaving only a small contingent of soldiers. Antigonus cultivated their friendship yet secretly hoped the Parthians would return and rescue him from the Romans.

He didn't know he soon would face a greater threat. Herod had sailed from Italy to Syria and landed at Ptolemais, a port city on the Mediterranean. He recruited an army of foreign and Jewish troops; most who joined hoped he would reward them after he'd secured his kingdom. With help from the Romans, he captured Joppa and rescued his family from Masada. He made an unsuccessful attempt to capture Jerusalem, even offering amnesty to the defenders, but Antigonus reminded his troops that Herod was an Idumean, a half Jew, not of the royal family. They refused to surrender.

After occupying Jericho and resupplying his troops, Herod led his army into Samaria and Galilee even though it was winter. He defeated forces loyal to Antigonus, except for roving bands of robbers who hid in near-impregnable caves and against whom he had to launch a second campaign. He designed chests connected to chains that allowed his soldiers to lower themselves over mountainsides and conduct assaults. In addition to their spears and arrows, they used grappling hooks to drag the bandits out of their enclaves.

After the first day of fighting, Herod offered amnesty to those who surrendered, but the robbers refused. Herod's soldiers started fires in the caves, and still they wouldn't surrender. The wife and children of one of the robbers pleaded with him to allow *them* to surrender; when he refused and they tried to give themselves up, he killed her and all seven children, threw them down the cliff, then leaped to his own death.

With additional help from Mark Anthony, Herod was finally ready for another assault on Jerusalem. After surrounding the city and getting the siege equipment in place, Herod put a general in charge and left for Samaria to marry Mariamne, a daughter of Aristobulus (the former high priest and ruler of Judea) and a Hasmonean. This obviously was a convenient political arrangement, strengthening Herod's claim to the throne. But Mariamne was also beautiful, and it seems that Herod truly loved her.

It took the Romans forty days to break through Jerusalem's outer walls, then fifteen more to capture the temple compound where Antigonus had taken refuge. Both Roman soldiers and Herod's Jewish troops, furious that capturing the city had taken so long, went on a rampage, slaughtering men and women, even infants and the elderly. Antigonus surrendered to stop the killing, yet still the Roman general was merciless. He ridiculed Antigonus, calling him by a woman's name (*Antigone,* in Greek, is a woman's name), then bound him in chains and took him to Anthony at Antioch in Syria. Because he was afraid Anthony might take Antigonus to Rome, where the deposed ruler might convince the Senate of his legal right to the throne, Herod paid Anthony to execute the last Hasmonean ruler. Antigonus was beheaded.

Internal squabbling, intrigue, and incompetence in the Hasmonean dynasty created an opportunity for the Herodians to gain control of Palestine.

After the last Hasmonean was dead, Herod finally had what he wanted. With Roman support, he was in complete control of Judea, his own kingdom. But the title "King of the Jews" didn't make Herod Israel's promised Messiah. Israel's true "King" and the world's Savior soon would be born in Bethlehem, a small, obscure town, seven miles south of Jerusalem.

The New Testament

The Jews and Roman Taxation

The Jews were accustomed to paying taxes. In addition to their own tithe and other religious offerings, through the centuries the Assyrians, Egyptians, Babylonians, and Persians had imposed heavy taxes on Israel and Judah.

During the Hellenistic era, the Greeks used a system of "tax farming," selling collection opportunities to the highest bidder. Herod the Great would utilize this arrangement as well. He placed levies on almost everything, taxing people on their land and crops, even their animals. They had to pay poll taxes, travel taxes, and sales tax on everything from food to slaves.

The tax burden was crushing under the Romans, who refined the method by requiring people to register in the town of their birth and by hiring chief collectors, who determined tax quotas and sold franchises to the highest bidder. (The trip Joseph made to Bethlehem [Luke 2:1–7] illustrates the requirement to register for a tax census in the place of birth.) Those who bought the franchises, known as publicans or tax farmers, generally were dishonest and greedy, cheating people by collecting even more than the government required, then keeping the rest for themselves.

Roman and Jewish troops enforced the payment of taxes. When John the Baptist began his ministry, he challenged people to repent and be baptized. When tax collectors and soldiers asked what they should do, John said to the former, "Don't collect any more than you are required to" and to the latter (probably Jewish soldiers of Herod Antipas—see chapter 7), he said, "Don't extort money . . . be content with your pay" (Luke 3:12–14).

The Jews loathed tax collectors. The occasion for the three parables in Luke 15 was the Pharisees' complaint that Jesus was eating with tax collectors and despicable sinners. In response to their criticism, Jesus, "a friend of tax collectors and sinners" (Luke 7:34; 15:1–2), told three stories about God's infinite, unconditional love for the lost.

Despite the Jews' prejudice, Jesus called Matthew, a tax collector, as one of his twelve apostles and then accepted an invitation to visit his home and meet his friends (Matthew 9:9–13). When the Pharisees criticized him for eating with tax collectors and other undesirables, he said it is "not the healthy who need a doctor, but the sick." He also commended Zacchaeus, a chief collector even more despised than those who worked for him. When Jesus invited himself to his home, Zacchaeus repented of his dishonesty, promising to repay those he'd cheated and to give generously to the poor. Jesus said he'd given evidence of genuine faith (Luke 19:1–10).

Jesus and Herod Antipas

Before Herod the Great died, he made his son Herod Antipas tetrarch of Galilee and Perea. This was the Herod who was infamous during the ministry of Jesus and who would kill John the Baptist.

When Jesus was in Perea, east of the Jordan River, a group of Pharisees warned him that Herod Antipas wanted to kill him. Jesus, who knew Jewish history as well as Jewish law, replied, "Go tell that fox, 'I will keep on driving out demons and healing people today and tomorrow, and on the third day I will reach my goal.' In any case, I must press on today and tomorrow and the next day—for surely no prophet can die outside Jerusalem!" (Luke 13:32–33). Probably he was referring to Herod the Great's execution of the notorious bandit Hezekiah; again, the Jewish law did not allow for capital punishment unless the high council in Jerusalem had reviewed the case. Jesus was reminding Antipas that to kill him without Sanhedrin approval would be to use his power illegally, just as his father had done.

Paul and a Roman Triumph

As we've seen, after he captured Jerusalem, Pompey took Aristobulus and other Jewish captives to parade them in his triumph. A victory parade in Rome was the highest honor that could be paid to a conquering general. To receive the honor, he had to lead his army in total victory against a foreign enemy force, not in civil conflict against other Roman troops. His soldiers had to kill or capture thousands of enemy troops and accumulate valuable spoils. The region had to be totally pacified, with additional territory coming under Roman rule.

For the actual procession, in which trumpeters, priests, and senate members also marched, the general rode in a chariot at the head of his troops, wearing a purple toga and holding a scepter bearing a Roman eagle. The priests waved incense burners, spreading victory's sweet fragrance to the soldiers and spectators. In contrast, to the enemy prisoners, shuffling along in chains, the smoky smell was the stench of death, as those who weren't slaughtered publicly would be sold into slavery.

Paul used the imagery of a Roman triumph to explain the paradox of victory in ministry *through* suffering and death. Through Christ, God has vanquished his enemies, yet Paul, now marching in the divine triumph, is Christ's *captive* (2 Corinthians 2:12–17; see also 1 Corinthians 4:9). The incense is the knowledge of Christ spread through the preaching of the gospel. *Aroma* is used for Old Testament sacrifices; thus Paul considers his life and the message the repugnant smell of death to those who reject the gospel and the sweet fragrance of life to those who accept Christ's once-for-all offering and receive him as Savior.

In a different context, Paul also uses the "triumph metaphor" to assure believers of God's victory over all diabolical "rulers and authorities" through the paradox of the cross (Colossians 2:15).

Questions for Discussion

1. The Romans gave Herod the title "King of the Jews." Discuss how and why he likely felt threatened when he learned about the birth of Jesus.

2. Discuss why the Jews despised the Herodians and refused to accept them as legitimate rulers.

3. Discuss the ways in which we can see God orchestrating history during the occupation of Judea by the Romans and the rule of Herod the Great.

4. What was the attitude of most Jews toward tax collectors (publicans)? Why?

5. Based on the example of Jesus, how are Christians to treat those who are loathed by others?

6. Describe a Roman triumph and discuss how that custom helps us in understanding 2 Corinthians 2:12–17 and 1 Corinthians 4:8–9.

6

"The Paranoid King"

The Roman Period: Part II

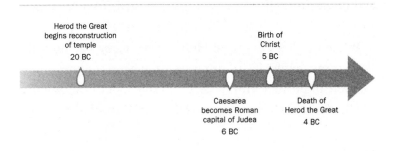

Herod the Great
begins reconstruction
of temple
20 BC

Birth of
Christ
5 BC

Caesarea
becomes Roman
capital of Judea
6 BC

Death of
Herod the Great
4 BC

Introduction

(AD 28: Jesus had begun his public ministry in AD 27. About a year and a half later, he was in Jerusalem with his disciples.)

Gazing upward, John exclaimed, "Isn't it *amazing*! Look at the size of those stones—how did Herod get those things all the way here from the quarry?"

"Well, the man was a crazy tyrant, but he was a genius when it came to building," said Peter.

(Source: Josephus, *Antiquities* 15.1–17.8)

121

"You're right," replied Simon. "Don't forget, though: Herod built this monument to himself, not to God, by the sweat and blood of Jews."

"Did you know he used his own personal funds for this, not money from taxes?" asked Matthew.

"Maybe," Thomas observed, "yet still this project has been going on for forty-six years. If an Idumean hadn't been in charge, it would have been finished in twenty."

Jesus had been quiet. "Master, what do you think of this?" Peter asked.

"See all these stones? I tell you the truth, every one of them will be overturned!" he answered (adapted from Matthew 24:1–2).

While the Jews despised Herod, they recognized his architectural genius. Jesus' disciples were no exception. They too were impressed with the size and splendor of the temple, which made Jesus' response puzzling. And troubling.

Herod and Alexandra

With the fall of Jerusalem, Herod the Great now controlled Judea, but he would discover that ruling a kingdom was more difficult than gaining its title.

He first attempted to consolidate power by rewarding supporters and eliminating opponents. He honored the Pharisee who'd defended him before the Sanhedrin (when he faced murder charges), and he executed the other members for daring to put him on trial. He plundered Jerusalem and sent great quantities of gold and silver to Mark Anthony at Antioch. Anthony had planned to take Antigonus, the former ruler and high priest, to Rome for his triumph, but when he was informed of the Jewish resistance to Herod and the continuing support for Antigonus, he ordered Antigonus beheaded. Herod knew the Jews would never accept an Idumean as their legitimate king, yet he made a clever attempt to gain their support. After the Parthians had captured the former high priest Hyrcanus, Antigonus had cut off his ears. Paying the Parthians to free Hyrcanus was risk free, as Herod knew the physically handicapped man could never again fulfill that role. Then to protect his rule even further, Herod appointed as high priest an old friend. Ananelus, a Jew who'd been living in Babylon, lacked political influence in Judea, so this was a safe appointment. Nevertheless, it was one that did not set well with Alexandra, the daughter of Hyrcanus.

Alexandra wanted the office conferred on her son, Aristobulus III, and wrote to Cleopatra, asking her to appeal to Mark Anthony. Anthony was hesitant only until he saw sketches of Alexandra and Aristobulus; she was beautiful, he was handsome. When he ordered Herod to install Aristobulus, Herod had no choice. Alexandra assured him she had no interest in political power—only in the priesthood—yet he suspected she was maneuvering to overthrow him.

And so Aristobulus wasn't high priest for long. Playing in a pool at his mother's house in Jericho, with one of Herod's servants, he mysteriously drowned. He was seventeen and had only served for one year. Herod denied any involvement and even mourned Aristobulus's death, but he didn't quell any doubts by immediately reinstalling his friend Ananelus as high priest.

Alexandra was deeply grieved and determined to get revenge. She told Cleopatra that Herod had murdered her son, and the queen again appealed to Anthony, charging that Herod was not fit to rule as king. In truth, she wanted Anthony to make Judea part of her Egyptian empire.

Anthony summoned Herod to Antioch to explain what had happened. Before leaving Judea, Herod put Joseph, his uncle and administrator, in charge of the kingdom and ordered him to *kill* his beautiful wife Mariamne if he did not return. Herod thought Anthony was in love with her, and he could not bear the thought of anyone else taking her as his wife.

Now in his absence, Joseph met often with Mariamne and Alexandra to discuss the affairs of the kingdom. On one occasion, he inadvertently revealed what Herod had ordered, were he to be executed by Anthony. Joseph explained that of course this was because of Herod's great love for Mariamne. Alexandra and Mariamne did not see it that way; in fact, they concluded that even if Herod were not killed he would somehow have them put to death.

Then a report came that Anthony had tortured and killed Herod. Alexandra was certain that if only he could *see* Mariamne he would give them the kingdom because of her irresistible beauty. But the report about Herod's death was false. The shrewd king had set the tone for the meeting with large quantities of silver and gold, gifts that spoke louder than Cleopatra's pleading and complaints. Anthony allowed Herod to return to Jerusalem. He also married Cleopatra VII, and gave her control of Syria, of the coastal area, and of several palm plantations near Jericho.

After Herod arrived, his sister and his mother (both of whom hated his wife) told him Joseph had been intimately involved with Mariamne. Though she was able to convince Herod the charge was false, she then let on that she knew of his contingent arrangement to have her killed. He blew up in a rage, convinced Joseph never would have revealed the plan unless he'd been intimate with her. His love for her kept him from killing Mariamne, but he ordered Joseph executed without a chance to defend himself. Sure that Alexandra was behind all this, Herod had her arrested and "kept in custody" (*Ant.* 15.3.9).

For her part, Cleopatra was not satisfied—she wanted more. And so she persuaded Malchus, the Nabatean king, to go to war against Herod. (Nabatea was an Arab country, located southeast of Judea.) Herod once again proved himself a skilled military leader, and even after suffering several costly defeats, he emerged the victor.

In another momentous struggle, Octavian, the man who would become Augustus Caesar, was grappling for control of the entire Roman Empire, and Cleopatra's dream of adding Judea to hers ended with Octavian's victory in the Battle of Actium. Anthony and Cleopatra retreated to Egypt, where they made a suicide pact. When Octavian's forces reached Alexandria, Anthony attempted to take his life with his own sword. He badly wounded himself but did not die immediately; his friends took him to Cleopatra's monument, where she was hiding, and he died in her arms.

Cleopatra then tried to charm Octavian. When she realized he intended to take her to Rome for his triumph, though, she tried to kill herself. She succeeded by allowing a deadly asp to bite her. (Possibly two bit her; small fang marks were found on her body.)

Herod, no matter how paranoid and unpredictable, was a wily politician. Having been a loyal Anthony supporter, he realized he had to act quickly. He met with Octavian on the island of Rhodes and succeeded in demonstrating his allegiance. He removed his crown for the meeting, actually boasted about his friendship with Anthony, and emphasized that even after Actium he had not abandoned but rather maintained his counsel, advising that he get rid of Cleopatra and make peace with Octavian. After he argued persuasively that such unwavering support was proof that he was an ally who could be trusted, the emperor-to-be reconfirmed him as king of Judea and placed even more territory under his control.

Herod would become one of Octavian's closest friends and supporters. When Octavian left Syria to invade Egypt, Herod gave him lavish gifts, and wine and water to sustain his army in the desert.

Herod and the Ghost of Mariamne

On returning to Judea, Herod found his kingdom and his marriage in jeopardy. Mariamne had become increasingly dissatisfied, suspecting that his love for her was only for the political advantage of her Hasmonean heritage.

Herod tried to show his love was true. To impress her, he told her he had convinced Caesar to allow him to remain king. But instead of rejoicing at the news, Mariamne resented his success and visibly showed her dissatisfaction.

Herod felt crazed with rage and wanted to punish or even kill her, yet couldn't because of his love for her. Sometimes he was able to convince himself he deeply loved her; but at other times she made him so angry he wanted to murder her. Always he was terrified that ordering her death would cause him unbearable grief.

Again Herod's sister and mother attempted to inflame his anger, but his fury was abated when he heard Octavian was victorious in Egypt and both Anthony and Cleopatra were dead. Ever the opportunist, he went to Egypt to congratulate Octavian, who rewarded him with the territories of Gadara, Hippos, and Samaria, along with several coastal cities.

Herod was proud of his accomplishments, yet Mariamne, as before, despised her husband. She openly criticized his mother and sister. Further, she refused to sleep with him.

Salome, Herod's sister, took advantage of his frustration and charged that Mariamne must have a secret lover. Then she persuaded his cupbearer to tell him that Mariamne had tried to poison him.

Herod ordered Mariamne's eunuch tortured, and while he knew nothing of any plot, he did reveal that another man, named Sohemus, was the one who'd told Mariamne of the plan to put her to death if Octavian executed him. Herod exploded in rage. He ordered Sohemus executed without trial and Mariamne seized and held for trial. She was given the opportunity to defend herself, but Salome convinced Herod to execute her. He ordered his beautiful wife put to death in 29 BC.

Mariamne might have lived a long and comfortable life as the favored wife of Herod. Ultimately, she was faithful to him, but she treated him rudely and publicly criticized his mother and sister. It seems understandable that she struggled to overcome the brutal fact of his having murdered her Hasmonean relatives.

After Mariamne's death, Herod suffered from such severe depression and guilt that he neglected his kingdom's administration and became delusional. When Judea endured a plague, he was certain it was God's judgment for his crime against his wife. He would order his servants to summon her as if she were still living. He made extended trips into the desert under the pretense he was hunting, but instead once there would punish himself. He developed severe headaches that his physicians could not help.

Alexandra, learning of his physical and mental incapacitation, conspired then to take over parts of Jerusalem. When some of Herod's supporters exposed her plans, he ordered her executed and was so paranoid he even had some of *his* closest friends likewise put to death because he thought they too were plotting to overthrow him. One had been Salome's former husband.

Herod, Callous King and (Nearly) Matchless Builder

Partly because he was ambitious and brilliant, and partly because he warily suspected nearly everyone to be plotting a kingdom takeover, Herod began an aggressive building program that included defensive fortifications.

Perhaps the most difficult challenge was the need to show respect for two cultures: Roman *and* Jewish. The customs and institutions of Roman society depended heavily on Greek culture; in many ways it was totally incompatible with Jewish traditions. Herod, who could not possibly rule as both a Roman and Jewish king, opted to give preference to the Romans. His decision inevitably would infuriate his Jewish subjects.

To honor Caesar, Herod built a theater in Jerusalem and an amphitheater for athletic games to be held every five years. He invited contestants from other nations, offering huge rewards to the winners. In the Greek custom, participants competed in the nude, a practice highly upsetting to the Jews. Men fought one another and fought wild animals and were rewarded with elaborate trophies. The Jews considered the gladiator contests inhumane, but most offensive were the trophies that they viewed as pagan idols.

Herod knew he was offending the Jews and tried to convince them the trophies were mere pieces of wood. He even showed a group of Jewish elders what they were before they were carved into trophies. When they weren't convinced, he went on to ridicule what he said was their foolishness.

Some Jews were so infuriated by what they thought was the king's deliberate disregard of their traditions that ten of them made a pact to kill him. Their plan to assassinate him at an athletic contest was foiled by a spy of Herod's, who warned him of the plot as he was entering the theater. When the people learned the identity of the spy, they tore him limb from limb and fed his body to the dogs. The Jews refused to reveal those who'd killed the spy, so Herod had some of the women involved tortured until they confessed, and then had the conspirators and their families brutally executed.

Even though he was a man of passion who'd rarely let anything stand between him and whatever he wanted, Herod likewise was shrewd enough to avoid infuriating the Jews when it was to his advantage. For example, he would learn that Simon Boethus, of the priestly line, had a lovely daughter, and when he saw her for the first time, he was overwhelmed with her beauty. He thought about just using her as he wished, but he knew well that such an abuse of power was likely to send the Jews into full-scale revolt. So he resolved to marry her, even though he considered her father to be of insufficient social standing; this "problem" he remedied by removing the high priest and installing Simon in his place. Having bequeathed to Simon the dignity of that office, Herod then married his daughter (his third wife, Mariamne II).

~~~~~

To strengthen his standing and protect his rule, Herod fortified his palace in Jerusalem. He also fortified the Akra and renamed it the Antonia Tower (after Anthony). He reinforced the city's walls with three defensive towers, strengthened the fortress at Masada, and built several other strongholds in Judea. He rewarded the Samaritans for their support by establishing Samaria as an independent state, expanding and fortifying their capital city, which he renamed *Sebaste* (Greek for *Augustus*), and building in its center a temple that he dedicated to Augustus.

One great accomplishment was the construction of a port on the Mediterranean Sea. After considering his options, says Josephus, Herod devised a plan for "a magnificent city" on the site of the ancient Phoenician harbor called Strato's Tower, a project that took between ten and twelve years to complete (*Ant.* 15.9.6). After the old harbor was dredged, Herod managed a feat of engineering (including the lowering of colossal limestone blocks into more than a hundred feet of water) that became the second-best harbor in the eastern Mediterranean (after Alexandria), a forty-acre port to accommodate three hundred ships. Herod renamed the city Caesarea, in honor of Augustus, and built a marble temple for worship of the emperor.

Herod built for himself a magnificent palace on a point that jutted out into the sea. For residents and visitors, he constructed a hippodrome, a theater, and a west-facing amphitheater that seated 3,500 and provided spectators a panoramic view of the Mediterranean.

The major drawback in location was the lack of fresh water. Herod solved this conundrum by constructing an aqueduct for transport from Mount Carmel, nearly ten miles away. To enable the flow of water by gravity, he had the aqueduct elevated on arches and the gradient carefully measured. Though Herod had built palaces and temples throughout Judea, in the eighteenth year of his reign he announced his intention to build "an everlasting memorial," and in 20 BC began a massive reconstruction and expansion of Zerubbabel's temple in Jerusalem. He wanted to make it one of the world's most magnificent temples, and he promised not only to use his own funds but also to construct it in a way that honored God.

For their part, the Jews were concerned that Herod would destroy the old temple and then never replace it. He was able to negotiate agreement by assuring the priests that sacrifices could continue during construction and that they could help with the work to ensure that nothing would be defiled. He kept his promise by employing a thousand priests as masons and carpenters.

The project began with turning Mount Moriah into a massive platform. Workers quarried stones from limestone deposits around Jerusalem and then used giant rollers to move them. Though smaller stones were used for the actual structure, the stones in the temple mount were massive. Some weighed over a hundred tons; one weighed almost six hundred tons (over a million pounds). The complex was constructed in levels, with each incrementally higher, so that the actual temple was the highest building in the complex. The temple proper was finished in a year and a half; work on the surrounding area continued for *eighty years*. Around the time of Jesus' public ministry, work had been ongoing for almost half a century (John 2:20).

Caesarea and the New Testament

Caesarea, about sixty-five miles west of Jerusalem on the Mediterranean coast, should be distinguished from Caesarea Philippi, twenty-five miles north of the Sea of Galilee. The Romans, taking direct control of Palestine in 6 BC, made Caesarea the province's political capital.

Though there's no biblical reference to the fact, Caesarea was undoubtedly the residence of the Roman governor Pontius Pilate. In 1961 archeologists discovered an inscription there with the name Pilate engraved on it.

After telling the Ethiopian eunuch the good news about Jesus Christ, Philip was taken to Azotus and preached the gospel from there all the way to Caesarea, a distance of sixty miles (Acts 8:26–40).

Cornelius, a Roman centurion and the first Gentile convert to Christianity, lived in Caesarea (Acts 10). Peter was in Joppa when the Lord revealed to him in a vision that the barrier of the Law, which had separated Jews from Gentiles, now was removed; Peter was free to go and proclaim the gospel to his household. When he shared the good news, Cornelius and his family believed in Christ and were baptized. This conversion became the precedent for proclaiming the gospel to Gentiles.

Herod Agrippa I resided in Jerusalem but used Caesarea as his capital. There the people of Tyre and Sidon sought an audience, as apparently the king had cut off their food supply due to their hostility toward him. Caesarea may have been a major source of their supply because its fresh water allowed for the growing of dates and grain in the area. When Agrippa appeared in his dazzling royal robes, the people worshiped him as a god, and when he accepted their worship and did not give honor to God, an angel of the Lord instantly struck him down. In Luke's words, "He was eaten by worms and died" (Acts 12:19–23). Josephus records that he was seized with violent intestinal pains and died within days (*Ant.* 19.8.2).

After Paul became a Christian, because of an attempt to kill him, the believers in Jerusalem put him on a ship at Caesarea that sailed to Tarsus (Acts 9:30). He passed through the city a second time on return from his second missionary journey (18:22). On his way to Jerusalem after his third journey, Paul arrived by ship at Caesarea and stayed at the house of Philip the evangelist (21:7–9). At Philip's home, the prophet Agabus symbolically bound Paul's hands and feet and predicted that he would be arrested in Jerusalem (21:10–16).

In Jerusalem, the Romans, thinking Paul had instigated a riot, arrested him, and learning he was a Roman citizen, placed him under protective custody. Because of an assassination plot, they secretly transferred him to the provincial capital (23:12–35), where the Romans believed they could better protect him. As a prisoner at Caesarea, Paul gave his testimony to Governor Felix and then to Governor Festus and King Agrippa II before his transfer to Rome to appear before Caesar (24:1–26:32).

Herod's Final Years

Toward the end of Herod's rule, both the hatred and intrigue in his family intensified. When he went to Rome to visit his sons, their hostility was visibly apparent. Aristobulus and Alexander made it publicly known that, once in power, they intended vengeance on those who'd plotted against their mother.

Salome, bent on getting rid of Mariamne's sons, started a vicious rumor in Jerusalem that the men aimed to kill the king. Increasingly concerned about his sons conspiring against him, Herod empowered Antipater, his son by his first wife, Doris. Then, when he could no longer ignore the whispers that they hated him, he had them arrested.

He requested and received Caesar's permission to try them. The two were put on trial and convicted, and Herod ordered them strangled to death. In the words of Josephus, such a "heavy crime" in his old age "was the action of a murderous mind and as such was not easily moved from that which was evil" (*Ant.* 16.11.8).

As Herod's own end neared, two pious and highly respected teachers of the Law realized he was dying and encouraged a group of Jewish boys to tear down the golden eagle he'd erected over the temple gate. They warned the young men it would be risky but assured them they would be honoring God and setting an example for posterity. When they received an erroneous report that the king had expired, the young men climbed up at midday and cut down the idol with axes.

Herod wasn't dead. He was so weak he could only lie on a couch, but he was filled with rage nonetheless. The boys were seized and brought before him, then taken to Jericho for trial. Herod ordered them as well as Matthias, one of the elderly instigators, to be burned alive.

Knowing that death was near and that almost no one would mourn for him, Herod summoned certain Jewish leaders to Jerusalem. He then had them arrested and held in the hippodrome. To ensure that there *would* be mourning, they were to be executed when he died.

Then Antipater, the son who'd brought false charges against Aristobulus and Alexander, ironically was victimized by similar slander, accused of plotting to poison his father. From his deathbed, Herod had him imprisoned. When the jailer informed him that Antipater had attempted to bribe him, Herod ordered him executed and buried in a common grave.

Such heartless acts of cruelty, especially against his own family, prompted Augustus's infamous quote. Herod apparently observed the laws of kosher and would not eat pork, so Caesar Augustus is supposed to have said, "I would rather be Herod's pig (*uios*) than his son (*huios*)." In Greek, the difference between *pig* and *son* is a single diacritical mark (').

In 4 BC, five days after Antipater's execution, Herod died of an intestinal disease, possibly cancer. He'd been in so much pain he'd considered suicide, but a cousin stayed his hand. Salome and his mother, Alexas, countermanded his order for slaying the Jewish elders, and the men were released. Archelaus, the son Herod had decreed would succeed him, made the burial arrangements, and Herod was entombed in the Herodium fortress near Jericho.

Three of Herod's remaining sons would rule following his death, though none as king. Archelaus (son of Herod's Samaritan wife, Malthace), whom Augustus thereafter would decree incompetent, became ethnarch of Judea, Samaria, and

Idumea; Antipas (the "Herod" later prominent in the Gospels, also the son of Malthace) became tetrarch of Galilee and Perea (Transjordan); and Philip (son of Herod's wife known as Cleopatra of Jerusalem) became tetrarch of Gaulonitis (Golan), Trachonitis (northeast of the Sea of Galilee), Iturea, and Paneas (Caesarea Philippi).

Conclusion

When Jesus was born, Israel was a Roman province ruled by Herod the Great. Rome had given Herod the title "King of the Jews"; the Jews refused to accept or honor an Idumean who was no descendant of David.

But no one living in first-century Palestine could have escaped the influence of Herod's rule. His cities, temples, palaces, seaports, aqueducts, amphitheaters, and fortresses seemed to be everywhere. His reconstruction and expansion of the temple in Jerusalem made it one of the ancient world's true marvels.

By any standard, Herod was a highly successful military leader and shrewd politician. He was a survivor, able to negotiate crucial alliances with the Romans when they were engaged in internal power struggles and to avoid defeat by foreign nations when they threatened his rule.

In making a name for himself and impressing Rome, Herod infuriated orthodox Jews. He tried to maintain a balance between multiple cultures, but leaned heavily toward all things Greco-Roman, which pious Jews despised.

Herod lived a life of luxury. He seemed to have all a man could want, and yet he constantly was ill at ease and even tormented by suspicion, particularly that his supporters, even members of his own family, were plotting against him. He murdered two of his wives and three of his sons.

It is no surprise Herod felt threatened when wise men from the East came seeking "the King of the Jews." *He* was that king, even if not a single Jew recognized him as such. And it wasn't difficult for him to order the slaughter of all infants under age two in Bethlehem's vicinity. He'd found himself in—then fostered and furthered—an environment of violence his entire life.

From a human perspective, Herod was a ruthless tyrant. Still, God can accomplish his good purposes through evil human intentions and actions. It is unlikely national Israel would have survived Roman conquest and domination without Herod the Great—the Romans would probably have totally destroyed Israel and dispersed the Jews all over the world much sooner than they eventually did in AD 70. *God used Herod to preserve his chosen people and keep the nation intact until the time came for him to send his Son, the promised Messiah, the world's Savior.*

Herod the Great and the New Testament

Herod and the Birth of Jesus

Jesus was born in 5 BC, a year before Herod's death. Josephus gives no information on Herod's reaction to his birth, but the New Testament records the slaughter of all babies around Bethlehem. Matthew says wise men saw a star in the East and came to Judea to worship the king of the Jews. Herod, upon learning of their mission, asked them to tell him when they found the child, because he also wanted to worship him. Of course he was lying—he'd pitilessly eliminated

The World of Jesus

everyone he thought was a threat. After the men worshiped the infant Jesus and gave him gifts, an angel warned them and Joseph about Herod's murderous intent. They avoided him on their return, and Joseph led the family's escape to Egypt. When Herod saw he'd been bypassed, he ordered the Bethlehem massacre. The biblical account is entirely consistent with Josephus's portrayal of Herod as a paranoid, scheming murderer.

Herod's Temple

Around 965 BC Solomon built the first temple (1 Kings 6:1–38), which the Babylonians destroyed in 586 BC (2 Kings 25:8–12). In 516 BC, under Zerubbabel's leadership, the Jews who returned from exile completed the second temple (Ezra 6:13–15), which the Seleucid ruler Antiochus Epiphanes desecrated in 168 BC, igniting the Maccabean Revolt. Three years later, under Judas Maccabeus, the Jews expelled the Syrians from Jerusalem and rededicated the temple to the Lord. When Pompey conquered Jerusalem in 63 BC, Roman soldiers defiled it again.

The temple briefly came under Jewish control when the Parthians helped Antigonus against Herod. When he recaptured the city in 37 BC, his Roman aides damaged but did not totally destroy the temple. Later, in 20 BC, he began a massive reconstruction and extension of the whole complex. At the time of Jesus it was called "Herod's temple" (or "the second temple"). When he said, "Destroy this temple, and I will rebuild it in three days," the Jews mocked him, for, from their vantage, the powerful Herod already had been working on its renovation and expansion, and work continued for nearly half a century (John 2:20).

The temple figured prominently in the life of Jesus. He was dedicated in it (Luke 2:22–24). His parents went every year, and even as a boy his ability to discuss the law amazed the Jewish teachers there (2:45–47). He called the temple his Father's house, indicating that at an early age he knew God was his Father (2:49). The devil tempted him to jump off the temple (4:5–8).

Jesus drove out its money changers (19:45–46). The priests only allowed use of Jewish currency there, so worshipers had to exchange foreign currency; the location of the exchange (the Court of the Gentiles) and the exorbitant rates of exchange led him to charge the religious leaders with robbing God of his honor. During Passion Week, he taught in the temple complex (19:47–48), which is equivalent to someone today lecturing in the chamber where the Supreme Court meets, and the Jewish leaders disputed his authority (20:1–2).

The temple's structure was patterned after the tabernacle, with three separate areas. On the outermost, known as the Court of the Gentiles, there were no restrictions on who could enter, but there was a sign warning Gentiles to stay out of the inner court under penalty of death. The Holy Place (inner court) and the Holy of Holies (located within the Holy Place) were separated by a thick curtain. Only the high priest could enter the Holy of Holies, and only once a year, on the Day of Atonement. When Jesus died, that curtain was supernaturally torn from top to bottom (Matthew 27:51), signifying that access to God was now equally available to everyone.

~

As he had announced, Herod intended to make the temple an "everlasting memorial," and indeed it was an amazing feat of engineering. The white limestone blocks to expand the base of the actual building were gargantuan: thirty-seven feet long, twelve feet high, and eighteen feet wide. One stone weighed over four hundred tons. It is still not known exactly how the builders cut to size, moved, and set in place those massive stones.

The temple's main sanctuary was made of white marble, decorated with gold, and elevated on a higher level than the outer court. The central courtyard was surrounded by covered colonnades. The eastern section was named Solomon's Colonnade because it had been part of Solomon's temple. When Jesus was walking there, the Jews confronted him and demanded that he tell them if he was the Messiah (John 10:22–24). After the healing of the lame man, the people surrounded Peter and John there (Acts 3:10–11). The early Jewish Christians met there also (5:12).

In about AD 30, when Jesus surprised his disciples by declaring that "not one stone here will be left on another" (Matthew 24:2), he foretold the temple's cataclysmic destruction. The Romans who'd put Herod in power were the ones who destroyed his temple, fulfilling Jesus' prophecy in AD 70.

Questions for Discussion

1. Cleopatra VII took her own life; so apparently did Mark Anthony after his defeat by Octavian. Are there circumstances that justify suicide? Why or why not?

2. Whether or not and to what extent Herod loved Mariamne, why was his marriage to her politically expedient? Discuss the following question: "Are there reasons for marriage other than love?"

3. Discuss why you think Herod was haunted by "Mariamne's ghost" after ordering her death.

4. How does the date of Herod's death help determine the date of Christ's birth?

5. Why was Jesus' pledge to rebuild a destroyed temple in three days so shocking to those who heard it?

6. Do you agree or disagree with the view that Herod, a cruel and unpredictable tyrant, was used to fulfill God's promise to send the Messiah? Explain your answer.

7

Jesus and the Herodians

The Early Church and the Herodians

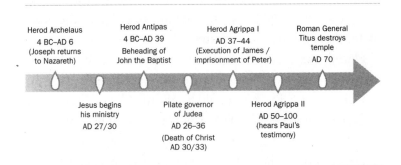

Herod Archelaus
4 BC–AD 6
(Joseph returns
to Nazareth)

Herod Antipas
4 BC–AD 39
Beheading of
John the Baptist

Herod Agrippa I
AD 37–44
(Execution of James /
imprisonment of Peter)

Roman General
Titus destroys
temple
AD 70

Jesus begins
his ministry
AD 27/30

Pilate governor
of Judea
AD 26–36
(Death of Christ
AD 30/33)

Herod Agrippa II
AD 50–100
(hears Paul's
testimony)

Introduction

(AD 28: John the Baptist had begun the ministry of preparing
Israel for Messiah's coming in AD 26. After about two years,
he was seized by Herod Antipas.)

After receiving the sealed notice a servant had brought from
the palace, Herodias went immediately to Salome. "Daughter,"
she said, "we have a special invitation. We will go to the king's

(Source: Josephus, *Antiquities* 18.1–20.11)

birthday party! And, Salome, he wants *you* to *dance*. You know he is a man of passions—you *must* excite him, for you are a beautiful girl. Who could know what he might give to you!"

Salome did dance. She danced alluringly, erotically. And she certainly excited him: Herod was so captivated he offered to give the girl anything she wanted, up to half his kingdom.

Herodias knew immediately she had a unique opportunity. She hated John the Baptist more than she could ever describe—because he had condemned her divorcing her husband, the king's half brother, to marry the king. And John was "available"; he was right there on the grounds, at the king's mercy, for Herod had imprisoned him. Herodias told Salome to go straight back to the king and request the head of John the Baptist on a platter.

Herod was caught completely by surprise. Instantly distressed (for he feared John), he deeply regretted his rash and foolish promise. But how could he afford to be so discredited in front of his guests? Everyone had heard what he'd pledged, and they all were right there, waiting, listening.

Herod ordered his soldiers to take off John's head.

In this chapter we'll survey Roman rule over Israel from around the birth of Christ (5 BC) to the destruction of the temple (AD 70). We will focus on the Herodian rulers who were important to the New Testament storyline.

The Life of Christ (5 BC–AD 30/33)

The Herodians

During the rule of Herod the Great (37–4 BC), the angel Gabriel announced to a priest named Zechariah that his wife, Elizabeth, would give birth to a son (Luke 1:5–25). Zechariah was instructed to name him John, and John's mission would be to prepare Israel for the Lord's coming.

Mary and Joseph were only engaged when Gabriel told her she would give birth to a son while still a virgin (1:26–46). He said God's Spirit would cause her to conceive miraculously so her child would be the Son of God.

Christ was born in 5 BC, near the end of Herod's rule, in the small village of Bethlehem (Matthew 2:1–12). When wise men came searching for the Messiah, the King of the Jews, Herod, in Jerusalem, asked them to report back to him so he too could worship the child. Herod had been given that very title by the Romans and feared the birth of a rival. An angel warned the men of Herod's deception, so after worshiping the child, they returned home without reporting back to him. When he discovered he'd been tricked, the king who'd killed two of his wives and three of his sons dispatched soldiers to kill every infant under age two in Bethlehem's vicinity.

The angel of the Lord informed Joseph and told him to flee to Egypt (2:13–17). While he, Mary, and Jesus were in Egypt, Herod the Great died.

When Herod died, Caesar Augustus divided his kingdom between three of his sons. Briefly: Archelaus, whom Herod thought would become king, received the title of "ethnarch" and ruled Judea; Antipas was made tetrarch of Galilee; Philip became tetrarch over areas northeast and east of the Sea of Galilee. All three are at least referenced in the New Testament.

Herod Archelaus (r. 4 BC–AD 6)

After the king's death, Archelaus, the oldest son, went to Rome anticipating he likewise would be installed as king.

He was unpleasantly surprised when Caesar only made him ethnarch (subordinate ruler) of Judea.

Archelaus apparently was ruthless too. Matthew says that when Joseph learned Archelaus now ruled Judea, he was afraid (2:22). An angel warned him about the danger, and from Egypt he brought the family instead to Nazareth, which was in Galilee but not in the jurisdiction of Archelaus.

Though Joseph's motive for going to live in Nazareth was to protect the child, this fulfilled the prophecy "He would be called a Nazarene" (2:23).

As it happened, Archelaus was so inept and unpopular that inside of a decade both Jews *and* Samaritans sent a delegation complaining about his rule. Caesar Augustus banished him to Gaul (which somewhat corresponds to modern France) and appointed Coponius, rather than another Herodian ruler, as governor (at the time, known as prefect).

Herod Antipas (r. 4 BC–AD 39)

Herod Antipas was appointed tetrarch (ruler of a fourth of a kingdom) of Galilee and Perea by Caesar Augustus, and he ruled for forty-three years. Like his father, he was an aggressive builder. He built several cities, including Tiberius on the Sea of Galilee, which he named in honor of Emperor Tiberius (AD 14–37) and made his capital.

When visiting Rome, Antipas stayed with his half brother, Herod Philip, a private citizen, and became romantically attached to his wife, Herodias. When he divorced his wife and married Herodias, John the Baptist condemned the marriage publicly because it violated the Law of Moses (Matthew 14:1–12). Herod had John arrested because he feared the prophet's denunciation might incite rioting (*Ant.* 18.5.2).

When Salome, daughter of Herodias, entertained Herod with an erotic dance, he excitedly vowed to give her anything she asked up to half his kingdom. Herodias used this chance to get rid of John, ordering Salome to ask for his severed head. Herod respected John as a man of God but granted the gruesome request and gave Salome his head on a silver platter.

Phasaelis, the wife Antipas had divorced for Herodias, was the daughter of Nabatea's King Aretas IV. Antipas and Aretas already had been at significant odds over issues of territory rights; the king's jettisoning of his daughter for another woman proved a last straw of sorts that resulted in a declaration of war on Antipas. When the Jews heard about the destruction of Herod's army by the Arab forces, they interpreted it as a divine judgment on his murder of John the Baptist (*Ant.* 18.5.1–2).

Though at one point some believed Jesus to be John the Baptist (or one of the prophets) returned from the dead, Antipas didn't; even so, he was puzzled by the reports about Jesus (Luke 9:7–9), who warned his followers to beware of the yeast of the Pharisees and of Herod (Mark 8:15). This was a figure of speech for a permeating evil; among other things, both Antipas and the Pharisees refused to recognize his miracles as evidence that he was Messiah. When a group of Pharisees warned him to leave Galilee because Herod wanted to kill him, Jesus called Herod a fox (Luke 13:31–35), a figure of speech implying Antipas to have been insignificant and destructive.

Though an Idumean (descendant of Esau), Herod Antipas was a practicing Jew. He was in Jerusalem for Passover when

Jesus was arrested and sent to Pilate (Luke 23:6–12). Not knowing what to do with Jesus, Pilate sent him to Herod because Jesus was from Galilee, in Herod's jurisdiction.

Herod anticipated an entertaining miracle. He asked Jesus numerous questions but was stymied and frustrated by his silence. He and his soldiers mocked Jesus, but in the end both Herod and Pilate maintained that he was innocent of any crime against Rome.

Previously between the two rulers there had been bad blood. Antipas and his brothers had once complained to Tiberius about Pilate's placing of Roman shields in Herod's palace, and Pilate had deeply resented the emperor's order to remove the shields. However, after the attempts to question Jesus, Antipas and Pilate settled their differences and became friends.

Later, Herodias urged her husband to petition the new emperor for a royal title. But his audience with Caligula was a disaster. A representative of Herod Agrippa I, Herod the Great's grandson, accused Antipas of treason, and Caligula banished him to Gaul, where he died (*Ant.* 18.7.2).

Herod Philip II, or Philip the Tetrarch (r. 4 BC–AD 34)

Philip, a just and competent ruler, was the half brother of Antipas, who was the son of Herod the Great and his fifth wife, Cleopatra of Jerusalem. He was tetrarch of areas east and northeast of Galilee (Luke 3:1), where few Jews lived; most of the population was Greek or Syrian.

One of Philip's notable accomplishments for the New Testament story was his building of Caesarea Philippi (not Caesarea on the Mediterranean) on the ancient site of Paneas.

It was there that Jesus asked his disciples this defining question: "Who do people say the Son of Man is?" Peter gave the answer he sought: "You are the Messiah, the Son of the living God" (Matthew 16:13–16).

When Caligula became emperor (AD 37), he gave Philip's former territories to Agrippa I.

The Birth and Growth of the Church (AD 30–96)

Herod Agrippa I (r. AD 37–44)

Agrippa I, the son of Aristobulus (son of Herod the Great) and Bernice, went to school in Rome. He never learned to master his passions, living licentiously and recklessly, piling up huge debts. Without paying what he owed, he returned to Palestine and was given a position in the government of Antipas, his brother-in-law. After Antipas criticized him as a freeloader, he went to live with the governor of Syria, another arrangement that didn't last long. Upon quarreling with Syria's governor, he returned to Rome.

Agrippa became the tutor of Caligula, Emperor Tiberius's grandson, and the two developed a friendship. At one point he made a truly careless but true-to-character remark, telling Caligula he should be the next emperor. When Tiberius heard what he'd said, he had him imprisoned.

Agrippa was very fortunate, though, because six months later Tiberius died. Caligula, now in fact the new emperor, freed him and gave him Philip's territory and the title of king. He returned again to Palestine in AD 23.

When Agrippa found out that his sister, Herodias, had convinced her husband, Herod Antipas, to ask for the title of king, he sent his own representative to Rome, where the man promptly accused Antipas of conspiracy. After Caligula banished Antipas to Gaul, he gave his former territories to Agrippa (*Ant.* 18.7.2).

In AD 41 Caligula was murdered, and Agrippa supported Claudius as the new emperor. In this he had supported the "right" man, and he was rewarded with Judea and Samaria. He now ruled over as much territory as had his grandfather, Herod the Great. But he wouldn't rule for long.

He tried to appease his Jewish subjects by persecuting Christians (Acts 12:1–23). He arrested and executed James. He arrested Peter and intended to execute him after the Feast of Unleavened Bread. After an angel miraculously released Peter, Agrippa had the guards put to death.

His reign and his life ended in AD 44, when a delegation came from Tyre to Caesarea. Agrippa, adorned in royal robes, gave a speech from his throne. Josephus says that when the people hailed him as a god, he saw an omen of his death, an owl sitting on a rope. He started suffering severe stomach pains, and he died five days later (*Ant.* 19.8.2). Luke records that because he refused to honor God and instead applied worship to himself, he was struck down by an angel of the Lord and eaten by worms (Acts 12:21–23).

Herod Agrippa I was survived by three daughters and one son, Agrippa II. One of his daughters, Drusilla, married Felix, who eventually became the Roman governor of Palestine. Agrippa II succeeded him as king.

Herod Agrippa II (r. AD 50–100)

Herod Agrippa II was in Rome when his father died. Because he was only seventeen, the emperor's closest advisors convinced the emperor not to give him the entire kingdom.

Roman Emperors

Augustus (31 BC–AD 14)

After defeating Mark Anthony in the Battle of Actium (31 BC), Octavian became the supreme ruler, and it was then that he took the name Augustus, "the exalted one."

When Jesus Christ was born, Augustus ruled the Roman Empire. He ordered the census that required Joseph to travel to Bethlehem to register for taxes (Luke 2:1).

He secured the empire's borders and brought in an era of unprecedented peace (known through the ages as the *Pax Romana*). Augustus reorganized the government and the legal system and engaged in an aggressive building program (including temples and roads). He established the imperial cult, the worship of Rome and its emperor, as the state religion. He did not require subjects to worship him as a god, but emperor worship would become a major threat to both Christians and Jews under Domitian.

To more effectively govern the vast empire, Augustus set up two types of provincial administration—senatorial and imperial. The Senate oversaw peaceful provinces and appointed each a proconsul. Acts says Gallio governed Achaia when the Jews accused Paul of breaking the Law (18:12–17). Gallio refused to hear the charges (they did not involve Roman law) and threw the Jews out of court.

Palestine, an imperial province, was administered by a military governor (prefect) directly responsible to the emperor. The New Testament mentions three: Pilate, Felix, and Festus.

Even though three Roman legions were totally annihilated in a futile attempt to expand into Germany, Augustus built Rome into a powerful empire.

Tiberius (AD 14–37)

When Augustus died, Tiberius, his adopted son, was chosen as emperor. He was generally disliked and executed those suspected of plotting against him. The New Testament refers to him by name only once (Luke 3:1). He was emperor during the life of Christ (20:22, 25), and when Christ was crucified (23:2).

Caligula (AD 37–41)

His given name was Gaius. But as a boy he marched around in military clothes and boots, so the soldiers nicknamed him *Caligula* ("little soldier's boot"). The Senate appointed him emperor after Tiberius died, and initially he was popular for reducing taxes and releasing political prisoners, including his friend Agrippa I, whom he gave the title of king and the territory of Herod Antipas.

Later in his rule, among other reckless (or even insane) actions, he even began demanding worship as a living god. He was assassinated by a group of imperial guards. He is not mentioned in the New Testament.

Claudius (AD 41–54)

Claudius was a surprising choice for emperor. A disease suffered in childhood left him drooling at the mouth and appearing mentally incompetent. This appearance was deceptive. He attempted to restore the regal credibility Gaius had severely damaged. He also expelled Jews, including Aquila and Priscilla, from Rome (Acts 18:2).

Nero (AD 54–68)

Claudius's wife, Agrippina, convinced him to make Nero, her son by another marriage, his legal heir. Then she poisoned Claudius.

When a disastrous fire swept through Rome, Nero blamed Christians. There was suspicion that he'd started the fire to make room for his palace and was diverting blame. But Christians were brutally attacked and murdered. Some were tied to poles, covered with pitch, set on fire, and used to provide light for orgies in the city. Others died in the arena, tied in the skins of slaughtered sheep and thrown in with wild dogs. It is believed that both Paul and Peter were executed during Nero's reign.

Nero fled Rome to escape a conspiracy, then later killed himself after learning the senate had ordered him seized.

Galba (AD 68–69)

After Nero died, the empire was divided by civil war. Galba, named emperor by the senate, was assassinated after seven months.

Vespasian (AD 69–79)

Vespasian came to rule through military power. While he was confronting the Jewish Revolt, the East's legions and provinces declared their support for him. He placed his son Titus in charge there and returned to Rome.

Titus (AD 79–81)

As a general, Titus captured Jerusalem and destroyed the temple in AD 70. The four-month siege was horrendous. Titus crucified five hundred Jews daily in sight of the defenders on the walls, tortured prisoners, and sold others into slavery. Afterward, it took three more years to capture Masada. After he became emperor, Titus died of fever after ruling only three years.

Domitian (AD 81–96)

Though emperor worship was part of Roman religious practice, Domitian, Titus's infamous brother, was the first to require everyone to worship him as a god. Both Jews and Christians were labeled "atheists" because they refused to participate in the imperial cult; he unleashed violent persecution of both. The apostle John recorded the book of Revelation to encourage Christians persecuted for their refusal to worship Domitian. He was assassinated.

Roman Governors

After Augustus banished Herod Archelaus to Gaul, the Romans placed Judea under control of a military governor. From then (AD 6) until the temple's destruction (AD 70), thirteen military governors ruled Palestine. Three are referenced in Scripture.

Pilate

Pontius Pilate (r. AD 26–36) ordered Jesus crucified. The Jews wanted him condemned as a criminal and executed, so they brought him before Pilate and insisted that the governor crucify him (Mark 15:1–15). Tiberius recalled Pilate to Rome because he slaughtered a group of Samaritans gathered at Mount Gerizim. He thought they were organizing an insurrection, but they only planned to search for a treasure they thought was hidden there.

Felix

Felix (AD 52–59) was a former slave who'd risen through the ranks to become a prefect. Appointed by Claudius, he was notoriously violent and corrupt. The Jews despised him and considered his marriage to his third wife unlawful. (He'd persuaded Drusilla, the Jewish daughter of Herod Agrippa I and former wife to King Azizus of Emessa, to divorce her husband and marry him, a violation of the Law.) Also, the Zealots began formally opposing Roman rule during his governorship.

When the Jews said Paul was inciting a riot in Jerusalem, the Romans arrested him and discovered he was a Roman citizen. They transferred him to Caesarea, the provincial capital, because of an assassination plot. Then the Jews hired Tertullus, an attorney, to bring charges against him before Felix, and his attempt to patronize the governor is apparent in his opening statement. Tertullus thanked Felix for his peaceful and just rule (Acts 24:2–4), an absolute lie. Paul made his defense and challenged Felix and Drusilla with the claims of the gospel. Felix refused to make a decision because he hoped Paul would pay him a bribe for his freedom (24:24–26).

Nero eventually recalled Felix to Rome, and Festus replaced him as Judea's governor.

Festus

According to Josephus, Festus (r. AD 59–62) was a fair ruler who tried to bring peace to Judea (*Jewish War* 2.14.1) by destroying bands of robbers called *sicarii* (*Ant.* 20.8.10). These "dagger men" kept short, sharp swords (knives) in their robes for robbing and killing Roman sympathizers.

In Luke's extended account of Paul's defense (Acts 25:1–26:32), after Festus arrived in Caesarea, he went to Jerusalem. The Jewish leaders asked him to return Paul there because they planned to ambush him. Festus denied them and said they'd have to come to Caesarea to make charges. He was following Roman law by requiring Paul's accusers to make a face-to-face legal indictment.

Several days later, the leaders arrived in Caesarea and made serious accusations without any evidence. Wanting to please the Jews, Festus agreed to return Paul to Jerusalem. Knowing he'd probably never make it, Paul used his citizenship to make an appeal to Caesar.

After conferring with his advisors, Festus agreed to send Paul to Rome; however, he didn't know how to charge him. When Agrippa II and Bernice arrived to pay their respects to the new governor, Festus asked them to hear Paul's defense. Again Paul used his circumstances as an opportunity to present the gospel to those present. In response to the witness of his miraculous conversion and apostolic calling, Festus concluded that Paul was a madman; Agrippa said it was ridiculous that he should become a Christian because of Paul's brief testimony.

Six years passed before Claudius made Agrippa II the king of Chalcis, his uncle's kingdom. Three years later Claudius gave him the territory of Philip in exchange for Chalcis, and then, after Claudius died, Nero, his successor, also gave him parts of Galilee and Perea.

When the husband of his sister, Bernice, died, she moved in with him. Agrippa and Bernice were suspected of incest by both the Jews and Romans; she persuaded King Polemo of Cilicia to be circumcised and marry her, but the union didn't last. She divorced him and moved back in with her brother.

Agrippa II asked Nero for authority over the temple, its treasury, and the appointment of the high priest (*Ant.* 20.1.3). The emperor granted his requests, and he retained this authority until the Romans destroyed the temple in AD 70.

Because of his familiarity with Jewish traditions, the Romans often sought the advice of Herod Agrippa II on religious matters. That explains why Festus, Judea's newly appointed governor, asked him to hear Paul's defense (Acts 25:1–26:32). And Bernice, then living with Agrippa, would explain why she came with him to pay respects to Festus (25:13).

After his defense, which included an emphasis on Jesus' death and resurrection, Paul indirectly challenged both Festus and Agrippa to believe on Christ. Festus responded by charging that Paul was crazy, and Agrippa made the cryptic statement, "Do you think you can persuade me to become a Christian so quickly?" (26:28 NLT). They agreed that Paul was not a criminal and could have been freed had he not made an appeal to Caesar (26:32).

Agrippa apparently knew that the Jews had no chance of defeating the Romans. He tried unsuccessfully to prevent the Jewish Revolt (started in AD 66). Though he kept Jewish customs, Agrippa sided with the Romans and eventually was rewarded with additional territory by the emperor Vespasian.

Bernice became the mistress of Titus, the Roman general charged with putting down the revolt. Titus also spearheaded the siege of Jerusalem, ultimately destroying the city and the temple in AD 70. Bernice lived with him during the conflict and went with him when he returned to Rome. She alienated the Romans by her arrogance and extravagant lifestyle, so Titus sent her back to Palestine. She returned to Rome after he became emperor; but Titus refused to get involved and once again sent her back to Palestine.

The Herodian dynasty came to an end when Agrippa II died in AD 100.

Questions for Discussion

1. Discuss the circumstances for the execution of John the Baptist. Why did Herod make such a rash promise to Salome? Do you think he was surprised when she asked for John's head? After she made her request, what would you have advised him to do, and why?

2. Regarding Herod Agrippa I's death, discuss whether or not you think the accounts of Luke (in Acts) and Josephus are contradictory.

3. Discuss the implications of the imperial cult for Christians, especially for Christians addressed in the book of Revelation.

4. Why did Rome appoint a governor to rule Palestine? Which three such governors does the New Testament mention?

5. Discuss the difference between a senatorial province and an imperial province. What kind was Palestine, and why?

6. Why did Nero blame Christians for the fire that destroyed large parts of Rome? Discuss what happened to Christians because of his charges.

7. Describe the political background for Paul's statement in 2 Timothy 4:6–8. How did he describe his impending death? Discuss his confidence that the Lord would judge him justly.

8

When Religion
Gets Sick

Years ago I read a book on pastoral care called *When
Religion Gets Sick*. The author, Wayne Oates, explained
what happens when faith becomes excessively judgmental
and legalistic. Though it would be foolish to attempt a psy-
chological analysis of the impact of Hellenism on Judaism,
that book's title appropriately describes what happened
spiritually to Israel in the four hundred years "between the
Testaments."

The coming of Hellenism threatened Judaism's future.
How could the Jews remain a separate people, chosen by
God, and not be assimilated into the nations? How could
they preserve a way of life based on the Law without becoming a Hellenistic cult? How could they submit to the rule
of foreign powers without giving up their trust that God
would intervene to vindicate them and deliver them from
their oppressors?

The religious groups and political parties at the time
of Christ reflected divergent responses to Hellenism. Not

all the responses were bad, but in their attempt to adapt to Greek influences and Roman and Herodian rule, most of them substituted materialism and nationalism for an authentic relationship with God. They covered over their lust for money and power with a veneer of spirituality. Instead of looking for a Savior who would save them from their sins, they longed for a king who would lead them in triumphant vengeance over the Romans and establish a political kingdom.

For others, however, foreign domination re-ignited their expectations for divine intervention. They correctly interpreted the Old Testament Scriptures and were confident that the Lord would keep his word to his people and to the world. They eagerly anticipated a Messiah who would deliver them from themselves. The Savior would overthrow Satan's rule and establish a universal kingdom of peace and righteousness that was open to everyone.

Religious "Parties"

Josephus identifies "three sects of philosophy": the Sadducees, the Pharisees, and the Essenes (*Ant.* 18.1.2). In addition to these groups, the New Testament identifies two others: the scribes and the Zealots.

The Scribes

The scribes were a professional group of scholars who interpreted the Scriptures and applied their teaching to daily life. According to Jewish tradition, Ezra was the first. To minister to the Jews who returned from exile, Ezra devoted himself to studying, obeying, and teaching God's Law. This tradition of interpreting and applying the Law continued until the time of Christ.

Though not a religious party, most scribes belonged to the party of the Pharisees (see Matthew 23:2). A few were connected with the Sadducees (see 2:4; 21:15). The expression "chief priests" also connotes some scribes being Sadducees, for they controlled temple worship.

As experts in case law, the scribes made legal decisions about the Law's application to daily life. For example, on Tuesday of Passion Week, the Pharisees, Herodians, and Sadducees tried to trap Jesus with embarrassing questions. One Pharisee, also a scribe, asked, "Of all the commandments, which is the most important?" (Mark 12:28). This was difficult, since there were hundreds and hundreds of negative and positive commands. But the scribe was impressed with his answer: "Love God and show your love for God by loving your neighbor" (12:29–33, author's paraphrase).

By the time of Jesus, the endeavor to interpret and apply the Law within Greco-Roman culture had resulted in a massive tangle of oral traditions. Jesus considered many of these a burden and a barrier between people and God. He faulted the scribes and Pharisees for their misuse of the Law and condemned them as "hypocrites" and "blind guides" (see Matthew 23).

A scribe was considered a teacher and often was called *rabbi,* a term of respect. Scribes had disciples who literally followed them and learned by memorizing their teaching and observing their lifestyle. The custom was for a disciple to choose a rabbi to follow; Jesus reversed the practice and chose twelve men to follow him. He had other disciples, but the Twelve had a special relationship with him.

The Sadducees

The name *Sadducee* was derived from Zadok, who was chosen as high priest after Solomon dismissed Abiathar (1 Kings 2:27; 4:2).

For the priestly aristocracy and secular nobility, the solution to the dilemma of Jewish uniqueness and Hellenistic eminence was some degree of compromise. During the Hasmonean Period they took control of the temple, making it and the sacrificial system their primary concern. They were willing to cooperate with corrupt priest-kings and brutal Roman prefects to protect their privileged status. Though less numerous than the Pharisees, under the Herodians they were the most powerful religious party.

They recognized only the authority of the Torah (the first five Old Testament books) and rejected the scribes' oral law. Their limited view of the Scriptures led them to deny the existence of spirits, the resurrection, and life after death. They lived for the present and did not look for Messiah's coming.

A classic example of their willingness to compromise is their conspiracy with the Pharisees to get rid of Jesus. They considered him dangerous because he upset the status quo. They tried to trap him with a question about the resurrection, but he pointed out that even the part of the Old Testament they accepted as authoritative gave evidence of it. When the Lord appeared to Moses, he said, "I *am* . . . the God of Abraham, the God of Isaac and the God of Jacob" (Exodus 3:6). They had died centuries earlier; the Lord's use of the present tense demonstrated the reality that life does not end here.

Christ's first followers proclaimed his resurrection, so Sadducees were the early church's primary opponents (see Acts

4:1–22). And because their primary focus was the temple, they disappeared after its destruction in AD 70.

The Pharisees

Pharisee comes from an Aramaic word meaning "to separate." They first appeared shortly after the Maccabean Period and were recognized as a religious group during the time of John Hyrcanus (135–104 BC). The group's response to Hellenism was to separate themselves from everyone and everything they considered unclean.

Descendants of the Hasidim ("pious ones"), Pharisees were passionately zealous for the Law. Though not a militant group, they joined the Maccabees in revolt against Antiochus Epiphanes because of his attempt to wipe out Judaism. After independence, they refocused on spiritual matters and the people respected them for honoring God through strict observance of the Law.

They believed the entire Old Testament (the Law, the Prophets, and the Writings) and their own oral traditions were equally authoritative. Against the Sadducees' naturalistic theology, Pharisees believed in a bodily resurrection, a future judgment, and the existence of spirits. They believed the future of God's people was tied to exacting adherence to the written Law and the oral traditions. They tithed, practiced prayer and fasting, and observed the Sabbath meticulously. They believed the keeping of the Law to the minutest detail would hasten Messiah's coming and bring rewards for their good deeds.

Though only numbering in the thousands, the Pharisees were extremely influential. Israel's religious "watchdogs" hounded Jesus for, in their opinion, ignoring the Law. They protested when he healed on the Sabbath (Mark 3:1–6) and when his disciples picked heads of grain while walking through grainfields on the Sabbath (Matthew 12:1–2). And because he ignored their traditions, the Pharisees and scribes branded Jesus a false prophet and plotted to kill him (John 7:25–52).

Somewhat uncharacteristically, he sternly denounced the Pharisees as hypocrites and warned them of severe judgment (Matthew 23:1–39). Not all Pharisees were hypocrites; some were sincere (e.g., John 3:1–15). Nicodemus objected to the unfounded conclusion that Jesus was a false Messiah (7:50–51), and helped Joseph of Arimathea give him a royal burial (19:38–42). Paul was a Pharisee who did his best to honor God by keeping the Law (Philippians 3:1–6). When brought before the Sanhedrin, realizing he would not get a fair hearing, he disrupted the proceedings by instigating a violent argument between Pharisees and Sadducees over the resurrection (Acts 23:1–11).

The Zealots

The Zealots were similar to the Pharisees in opposing Hellenism, but they also openly believed in using violence for the cause of religious freedom and in full-scale war for the cause of independence. They were eager recruits for the Maccabean revolt, and though their nationalistic fervor subsided some during the Hasmonean era, Roman occupation rekindled those fires. Unlike the Pharisees, who believed Roman domination was punishment for sin and were willing to wait for God to deliver them from oppression, the Zealots took matters into their own hands.

The movement initially began when certain patriots escalated the struggle for religious freedom into a war for independence from the Seleucids. During the rule of Herod the Great, the Romans sent Coponius to govern Israel and Quirinius to register the Jews for taxes (Luke 2:2). Though the high priest urged the nation to comply, a rebel leader named Judas started a resistance movement. He convinced others to submit only to the rule of God (*Ant.* 18.1.1). They refused to pay taxes, opposed the use of the Greek language, and engaged in guerrilla warfare against the Romans.

Simon, one of Jesus' disciples, had been a Zealot (Luke 6:15; Acts 1:13). The Zealots may have been associated with the *sicarii*; the Roman officer who arrested Paul thought he might have been a member of such a band of assassins. He asked, "Aren't you the Egyptian who started a revolt and led four thousand terrorists out into the wilderness some time ago?" (Acts 21:38).

The Zealots can be admired for their patriotism, but Josephus questioned their place in history. He blamed them for one violent war after another and ultimately the temple's *and* the nation's destruction in AD 70 (*Ant.* 18.1.1).

The Essenes

Like the Pharisees, the Essenes believed in the importance of strict ritual purity, yet unlike the Pharisees, the Essenes considered the Hasmonean priest-kings so corrupt they withdrew from worship in the temple and the customary practice of Judaism. Many isolated themselves and lived together out in the Judean wilderness; many of these formed the Qumran community near the Dead Sea and were considered Israel's "righteous remnant."

The ascetic Essenes had strict rules for life within exclusive community. Some believed in marriage; many did not.

Instead, they adopted young boys to train them for the Essene life. They rejected private property, practicing communal resourcing, and expecting every member to work and to contribute.

The Essenes were utterly paranoid about ritual purity. If they came into contact with anything or anyone impure, or even if they thought they might have, they ceremonially cleansed again and again and again. The discovery of several large pits at Qumran with stairs leading in and out suggest these pits were pools, filled with water for ritual cleansing.

Like Ezra the scribe, who'd devoted himself to study, application, and teaching (Ezra 7:10), the Essenes studied and copied the Law. They so rigorously practiced and enforced the Law that they believed even the ultra-legalistic *Pharisees* to be corrupt, primarily because the Pharisees continued to worship in the temple.

Like many overzealous prophetic speakers today, the Essenes would not consider any alternative to the fact that they were living in the very "last days." They believed Messiah would return soon and lead them, "the sons of light," into holy war against "the sons of darkness."

The Essenes are not mentioned in the New Testament, though now and again someone has attempted to identify John the Baptist as an Essene. However, while John had disciples (John 3:23–26), he was a single prophet, not part of a community (Luke 7:24–28). John was a reformer, not a preacher of doom. And John's baptism was not about ceremonial washing—he exhorted Israel to be baptized and repent to avoid judgment (Mark 1:1–8).

Jesus was definitely not an Essene. The Essenes would have condemned his way of life and teaching. He sought out the kind of people Essenes avoided at any cost. He attended a party for tax collectors at Matthew's home; when he was criticized for eating with scum, he answered that he had come to save sinners (Matthew 9:10–13). He invited himself to dinner at the home of Zacchaeus, a chief tax collector (Luke 19:1–10). Instead of abandoning the temple, Jesus taught there (19:47–48). After his resurrection, Peter and John went to the temple to pray (Acts 3:1). Jesus harshly condemned the Pharisees' nitpicking interpretation of the Law (Matthew 23:1–36). He would have been even more adamantly opposed to the harsh perfectionism of the Essenes.

In the last revolt against Rome (AD 66–70), the Essenes at Qumran hid large numbers of their documents in caves near the northern end of the Dead Sea. A Bedouin shepherd discovered these documents, known as the "Dead Sea Scrolls," in 1947. While herding goats he found several jars containing leather scrolls. Over a period of years, additional scrolls were uncovered that contain the community's rules and beliefs; there also are copies of (in total) nearly the entire Old Testament, including a scroll of the complete book of Isaiah. The Dead Sea Scrolls, a remarkable find, have enabled scholars to confirm the accuracy of the Old Testament text and provided valuable insight into one form of Judaism (apocalyptic) at the time of Christ.

Conclusion

Some Jews enthusiastically embraced Hellenism; most resisted what they perceived to be a threat to their survival as God's chosen people.

The responses ranged from peaceful submission to violent resistance. The scribes immersed themselves in the study and application of the Law. The Sadducees accepted Roman rule to protect their privileged role as guardians of the temple. The Pharisees tried to honor God through strict observance. Others, like the Zealots, courageously defied the Romans and fought to overthrow their oppressors. The Essenes isolated themselves in communities and rigidly ordered their lives to protect their perception of purity.

Jesus endorsed none of these responses. He taught and challenged his followers to a different way of life: the way of love. He did not come to overthrow the Romans or to enforce a stricter application of the Mosaic Law but to show us the way to God. On the night before his crucifixion, he said to his disciples in the upper room, "I am the way and the truth and the life. No one comes to the Father except through me" (John 14:6).

Questions for Discussion

1. Discuss the different responses of Jews to the influence of Hellenism. How do you believe you would have responded to its advance?

2. Are there cultures that you believe are threats to the Judeo-Christian heritage of American values? Why or why not?

3. Of the various groups described in this chapter, which one might you have joined, and why?

4. Choose two passages from the four Gospels and discuss why the scribes and Pharisees were Christ's primary opponents.

5. Choose two passages from the book of Acts and discuss why the Sadducees emerged as the foremost antagonists of the early church.

6. In what ways are believers today like the following (comparisons can be both positive and negative):
   • scribes
   • Pharisees
   • Sadducees
   • Essenes

7. Discuss how becoming a follower of Christ changed Matthew, a tax collector, and Simon, a Zealot. Talk about how becoming a believer has changed you.

8. In contrast to how the Zealots responded to Roman rule, how does Scripture teach Christians to respond to government, particularly when its policies are antithetical to Christian beliefs and values?

Conclusion

In the Fullness of Time

The story of Israel between the Testaments is one of tragedy and hope.

The fall of Jerusalem in 586 BC was a disaster. The unthinkable had happened. After half a millennium Israel ceased to exist as a nation, the temple was reduced to a pile of rubble, and seemingly countless Jews were taken into exile. Judah became a Babylonian province. The messianic hope was an impossible dream. Without a national homeland, how could God send the Messiah?

Though it appeared he had abandoned his people, the prophets assured the exiles that the captivity would not last forever. God was faithful; he had not reneged and would not renege on his promises. After seventy years, the Persians conquered the Babylonians. King Cyrus issued a decree allowing the exiles to return to Judea. Thousands did. Under Zerubbabel, they rebuilt the temple, and then later with the help of Ezra and Nehemiah, they pledged to obey the Law of Moses. Hope was still alive.

The Persians controlled Israel for over two centuries, but the future of the Jews would be determined by events beyond their control. At age twenty, the son of Philip became the ruler of Greece. Under Alexander the Great's leadership, the Greeks conquered the vast Persian Empire and spread the Greek way of life from Egypt to India. Alexander did not invade and destroy Judea, yet the Jews could not resist the Hellenistic advance. They studied the Greek language and philosophy, and even adopted Greek dress and custom.

After Alexander's death, Israel came under the control of the Ptolemaic dynasty of Egypt and then the Seleucid dynasty of Syria. Under Ptolemaic rule, the Jews were permitted to worship the Lord and practice their traditional way of life. During the rule of Ptolemy Philadelphus, Jewish scholars in Alexandria translated the Hebrew Old Testament into the more popular Greek, making the Scriptures more accessible to Greek-speaking Jews.

The peaceable relationship with the ruling power changed drastically when the Seleucids defeated the Ptolemies in 198 BC. Israel came under Syrian control, which attempted to wipe out Judaism and force the Jews to accept Hellenism. Antiochus Epiphanes set up an altar to Zeus in the temple and violently persecuted anyone who refused to abandon Judaism.

The attempt to forcefully Hellenize the Jews backfired. Not yielding to the demands of Antiochus, the Jews rebelled. Under the sons of an aged priest from the village of Modin, the Maccabees conducted a guerrilla war against the Syrians and, against overwhelming odds, won their freedom. A new dynasty of priesthood was legitimized when Simon, last of the Maccabees and first non-Aaronic priest, was crowned ruler and high priest "forever."

When the Syrians recognized Israel during the rule of John Hyrcanus, the Jews finally had their independent state. But the religious life of the nation deteriorated and divided into two distinct political factions. The conservative-minded Jews (Hasidim) who opposed Hellenism became the Pharisees. Those willing to adopt "the Greek way of life" became Sadducees. The parties became bitter enemies, both trying to win the favor of the Hasmonean rulers. After the death of John Hyrcanus, the Hasmonean era was characterized by one divisive power struggle after another.

Rome, expanding its empire in the East, took note of the chaos in Israel. A civil war between Alexandra's sons provided the Romans their opportunity. Pompey invaded the divided and weakened state and captured Jerusalem in 63 BC. For his support, Herod Antipater, an Idumean, was appointed governor of Judea. Antipater appointed his sons Phasael and Herod regional rulers over Judea and Galilee. The Parthians killed Phasael when they attacked Jerusalem; Herod escaped to Rome and was given the title "King of the Jews." With Roman help, he invaded Judea and became a "client king." Known as Herod the Great for his building projects, he was an architectural genius. He transformed the temple into an ancient wonder and at Caesarea forged the second largest Mediterranean harbor. Though brilliant, he also was paranoid and cruel. He had three sons and two wives put to death on suspicion of treachery.

Though Israel now had a king, he was not a Davidic descendant, the promised Messiah, but a despised Idumean, a descendant of Esau. Still, God had not forgotten his promises. Unnoticed by the powerful Romans, the long-awaited messianic king was born in Bethlehem. When Herod learned of his birth, he felt so threatened he ordered the killing of all the babies there. An angel warned Joseph of the danger, and he took his family to Egypt. Hope was still alive. Herod died in 4 BC; his kingdom was divided among three sons.

Herod Archelaus was appointed ruler of Judea and Samaria but was banished to Gaul for incompetence. (Dissatisfied with their client kings, the Romans sent military governors to rule Judea. Pontius Pilate was governor during the life of Christ and ordered him put to death by crucifixion.) Herod Philip was made tetrarch of the northern area of his father's kingdom; Herod Antipas, tetrarch over Galilee and Perea, was denounced by John the Baptist for divorcing his own wife and marrying his brother's. At the request of his wife's daughter, he ordered John beheaded.

Two of Herod's descendants are mentioned in Acts. Herod Agrippa I ordered James executed and Peter arrested. When a delegation from Tyre worshiped him as a "god," he accepted their praise and was struck down by the Lord. Because he was new to Palestine and unfamiliar with Jewish traditions, the Roman governor Festus asked Herod Agrippa II to hear Paul's defense and make a recommendation about the charges against the apostle.

The Zealots continued armed resistance, and an unsuccessful rebellion in AD 66 resulted in the destruction of the temple in AD 70. After a second revolt (AD 135), the rebel leader was captured and executed. The Jewish people were dispersed and prohibited on penalty of death from returning to Jerusalem. A temple dedicated to Jupiter was built on the temple's previous site. National Israel had come to a tragic end, but hope was still alive.

After his death and resurrection, Jesus Christ commissioned his followers to go to all nations and preach the gospel. By the end of the first century, Christians numbered in the thousands, and churches had been established from Jerusalem to Rome. The world's King and Savior was and is alive! Though sometimes called "The Four Hundred Silent Years," the period between the Testaments was anything but silent. God was at work, not directly through the prophets, but providentially preparing the world for the coming of his Son. God's timing is always perfect. Jesus Christ was born at exactly the right time in history. In an outstanding work, David Breed wrote of the world's preparation for Christ's coming:

> Surely, then, it is the fullness of time. If the Redeemer is ever to come to Zion it does seem as if he must come now. If the deliverer is ever to be manifested to Israel it would seem that he must now appear. And indeed he has appeared! The angels have sung their songs over Bethlehem, and the decree of the deification of Augustus is promulgated at the point midway between the birth of the deliverer and his baptism. The final conflict is indeed inaugurated and the final victor is foreshadowed. By and by it will be acknowledged in the despairing cry of one of the last Roman emperors, "Nazarene! Thou hast conquered!" (*A History of the Preparation of the World for Christ*, 360–361).

"When the time was right, God sent his Son into the world, born of a woman, to redeem those condemned by the law of God, so that we might become children of God" (Galatians 4:4–5, author's paraphrase).

Glossary

Abomination of Desolation (168 BC)—the event that precipitated the Maccabean Revolt. Soldiers of the Seleucid ruler Antiochus Epiphanes invaded Jerusalem, dedicated the temple to the Greek god Zeus, and sacrificed unclean animals on the altar.

Akra—a fortress on a hill in Jerusalem, built and fortified by Antiochus Epiphanes. It was a threat to the Jews until Simon, a Maccabean leader, captured and destroyed it in 142 BC.

Alexander Jannaeus (r. 103–76 BC)—son of Aristobulus I; an ambitious and arrogant Hasmonean king. He took the surname *Alexander,* after Alexander the Great.

Alexander the Great (r. 336–323 BC)—son of Philip, king of Macedonia. After his father's death he conquered the Persians and established an empire extending to Egypt in the south and India in the east.

Alexandra—mother of Mariamne, mother-in-law of Herod the Great. She made friends with Cleopatra of Egypt, schemed to overthrow Herod, and ultimately was executed because Herod blamed her for his love/hate relationship with Mariamne.

Alexandra of Jerusalem (r. 76–67 BC)—also known as Salome Alexandra; the only woman to rule Israel. As a woman, she could not hold the position of high priest.

Alexandria—a city in Egypt established by Alexander the Great that became the leading commercial port on the eastern Mediterranean

Sea and a major educational center. Later it became the capital of the Egyptian (Ptolemaic) Empire; it was here that the Old Testament was translated into Greek (the Septuagint).

Antigonus (r. 40–37 BC)—last of the Hasmonean rulers and son of Aristobulus II. He asked the Roman senate to restore him to power; they made Herod Antipater governor instead. When the Parthians occupied Judea, they installed Antigonus as king, but he was later defeated, captured, and beheaded by the Romans.

Antioch—Unable to maintain his capital in Babylon, Antiochus II established Antioch, on the Mediterranean Sea, as capital of the Syrian (Seleucid) Empire. Paul and Barnabas taught new believers at Antioch, where believers in Jesus Christ were first called *Christians*.

Antiochus IV, "Epiphanes"—the most infamous Seleucid ruler (r. 175–164 BC); attempted to impose Hellenism on the Jews by violent persecution. Desecrated the temple in 168 BC, an act of abomination that ignited the Maccabean Revolt. The Jews nicknamed him *Epimanes*, a play on *Epiphanes* meaning "madman."

Aramaic—the language of the Babylonians. As a result of the exile, many Jews adopted it as their preferred language. Jesus spoke Aramaic, Hebrew, and Greek.

Aristobulus I (r. 104–103 BC)—the second Hasmonean ruler; declared himself king but ruled only one year. He was insanely suspicious of everyone, including his family.

Aristobulus II (r. 67–63 BC)—Hasmonean ruler whose struggle for control with his brother, Hyrcanus II, gave the Romans the opportunity to conquer Judea.

Babylonia—the empire that controlled western Asia and, in 586 BC, conquered Judea. Under Nebuchadnezzar, the Babylonians three times invaded Judah, the third time capturing Jerusalem, looting and destroying the temple, and taking thousands of captives to Babylon.

Battle of Paneas (198 BC)—The Syrian (Seleucid) ruler Antiochus III, known as "the Great," defeated the Egyptians (Ptolemies) at Panium, near the headwaters of the Jordan River, and wrested control of Palestine, which the Seleucids would hold up to the Maccabean Revolt and the subsequent Hasmonean era.

Glossary

Bernice—sister of Agrippa II; mistress of Titus. Along with her brother, she heard the apostle Paul's defense before Governor Festus.

Caesarea—the second-largest seaport in the eastern Mediterranean, built by Herod the Great and named after Caesar Augustus. For that region, the Romans made Caesarea, rather than Jerusalem, their political capital.

Cleopatra VII—Queen of Egypt and lover of Mark Anthony. She sought to expand Egyptian power into Judea, but after Anthony's defeat she took her own life.

Cyrus (r. 559–530 BC)—Persian king known as "the Great"; after conquering the Babylonian Empire, he issued a decree allowing exiled Jews to return to Judea.

Daniel—a prophet taken hostage and brought to Babylon after the first invasion of Judea. He counseled three Babylonian kings and Cyrus king of Persia; he also prophesied about the rise and fall of empires, from Babylon to the establishing of God's kingdom.

Darius I (r. 521–486 BC)—Enemies of the Jews stopped the rebuilding of the temple during his reign over the Persian Empire; after a search of the archives for Cyrus's decree, Darius ordered the governor to permit the project *and* to provide building materials for it. Zerubbabel's temple was completed during his rule in 515 BC.

Demetrius I (r. 162–150 BC)—nephew of Antiochus Epiphanes, Seleucid (Syrian) ruler. His forces outnumbered and killed Judas Maccabeus.

Diaspora—collective term referring to Jews who lived outside Palestine. As a result of the Babylonian exile, the conquests of Alexander the Great, the persecution of Antiochus Epiphanes, and the advance of the Roman Empire, Jews were dispersed throughout the ancient Near East.

Ezekiel—Like Daniel, Ezekiel prophesied during the seventy-year exile. His ministry was primarily to the common people rather than to rulers.

Ezra—scribe and priest who led the second and smaller group of returnees back to Jerusalem in 458 BC. His ministry was focused on the study and teaching of the Law.

Feast of Dedication (also Feast of Lights or Hanukkah)—annual celebration of how, in 168 BC, Judas and the Maccabees defeated the Syrians and recaptured Jerusalem, then cleansed the temple and rededicated it to the Lord.

Felix (r. AD 52–59)—Roman military governor of Judea, despised by the Jews for his corruption. Some Jews brought charges against Paul before Felix at Caesarea.

Festus (r. AD 59–62)—Roman military governor of Judea who replaced Felix and, after hearing his defense, granted Paul's request to appear in Rome before Caesar.

Hasidim—the "pious ones." A term used in 1 Maccabees to describe Jews who held tenaciously to traditions and the Law of Moses and who strongly opposed Greek rule and culture. They are believed to be the forerunners of the Pharisees.

Hasmonean—the Jewish dynasty that emerged from the struggle for independence. It is thought the name was derived from Hashmon, an ancestor of the Maccabees.

Hellenism—term used to describe the Greek culture and way of life. Alexander and his successors established Hellenism in the nations they conquered and ruled.

Herod Agrippa I (r. AD 37–44)—grandson of Herod the Great; ruled over Judea and Samaria and was given the title *king*. Agrippa I, who attempted to appease the Jews by imprisoning the apostle Peter and by executing the apostle James, was struck down by an angel of the Lord when he accepted worship offered by a delegation from Tyre.

Herod Agrippa II (r. AD 50–100)—son of Herod Agrippa I, believed to have had an incestuous relationship with his sister Bernice. He and Bernice heard Paul's testimony at Caesarea, with Agrippa flippantly dismissing Paul's testimony about Christ while also concluding that Paul had not violated Roman law.

Herod Antipas (r. 4 BC—AD 39)—tetrarch (ruler) of Galilee and Perea; a son of Herod the Great and an aggressive builder like his father. After John the Baptist condemned his marriage to Herodias, the wife of his half brother Herod Philip, Herodias connived to compel him to execute John by beheading.

Herod Antipater—ruler of Idumea; father of Herod the Great. For supporting the Romans, he was appointed as Judea's administrator in 48 BC.

Herod Archelaus (r. 4 BC–AD 6)—eldest son of Herod the Great; made ruler of Judea after his father's death. After taking refuge in Egypt, Joseph returned with Mary and Jesus to Galilee rather than Judea in order to avoid Archelaus.

Herod the Great (r. 37–4 BC)—ruler of Judea. After escaping the Parthians, Herod fled to Rome, where the Senate surprised him by conferring the title "King of the Jews." He was brilliant and cunning but paranoid and ruthless; he ordered the killing of all infants around Bethlehem to ensure that he killed Jesus, the Jews' true king.

Idumeans—the descendants of Esau who inhabited an area southeast of the Dead Sea. The Herodians, who were patron rulers of Judea under the Romans, were Idumeans and were held in contempt by the Jews because of their lineage.

Jerusalem—the capital of Israel. After he became king, David made Jerusalem Israel's political and religious capital.

Jeshua—high priest in Jerusalem after the first return from the Babylonian exile, in 538 BC. He and Zerubbabel, the group's civil leader, organized the returnees for the rebuilding of the temple.

John Hyrcanus (r. 135–104 BC)—first of the Hasmonean rulers after the death of Simon, last of the Maccabeans. When he was criticized by the Pharisees, Hyrcanus joined the party of the Sadducees.

Jonathan—son of Mattathias and second leader of the Maccabees, he gained recognition for the Maccabees as a legitimate political party in Israel and for himself as high priest, though he was not in the lineage of Zadok. He was captured in an ambush and later executed by the Syrians.

Judas Maccabeus—oldest son of Mattathias and first leader of the Maccabean Revolt. For his courage and his stunning victories over the Syrians, Judas was given the nickname *Maccabeus*, probably from a word for "hammer." He was killed in battle.

Malchus—Nabatean king convinced by Cleopatra to go to war with Herod the Great.

Mariamne—the beautiful Hasmonean wife of Herod the Great. They had a love-hate relationship, and in the end he had her put to death.

Mark Anthony—Roman general and lover of Cleopatra. He considered Herod the Great an ally and helped him gain the title King of the Jews. Anthony was defeated by Octavian (Caesar Augustus) at the Battle of Actium and was severely wounded. He then apparently committed suicide to avoid capture.

Mattathias—high priest in the village of Modin. When a Syrian envoy ordered Jews to sacrifice to the Greek gods, Mattathias killed both a Jew who tried to sacrifice and the envoy. His bold and courageous act started the Maccabean Revolt.

Modin—a small village north of Jerusalem, where the Maccabean Revolt began.

Nabatea—an Arab country located south of Judea.

Nebuchadnezzar—king of the Babylonian Empire (r. 605–552 BC) whose army invaded Judah three times. On the third invasion (586 BC), he captured Jerusalem, sacked the temple, and deported thousands of Jews.

Nehemiah—cupbearer and advisor to the Persian king Artaxerxes I. He received the king's permission to go to Judea and organize the rebuilding of the wall of Jerusalem in 444 BC.

Octavian (Caesar Augustus)—ruler of the Roman Empire when Jesus was born; became emperor after defeating Mark Anthony. An excellent administrator, he organized the empire into senatorial and imperial provinces. The imperial cult (worship of the emperor) was started under his rule.

Parthians—a powerful empire in the East (Iran), they rose to power in the mid-third century BC when they revolted against the Seleucids. They expanded west to the Euphrates River, which became their boundary up against the Roman Empire. They occupied Jerusalem briefly during the Roman period; Herod the Great escaped, but they killed his brother Phasael. Though driven out of Judea shortly thereafter, the Parthians remained a threat to Rome until Trajan defeated them (AD 114–116).

Glossary

Paul—a former Pharisee who, after being miraculously converted on the road to Damascus, became a champion of the Christian faith. Called as an apostle, Paul traveled throughout the Roman Empire preaching the gospel and writing epistles (letters) to the young churches. He was executed by the Romans in the AD 60s.

Persia—the empire that conquered the Babylonians. In 539 BC, King Cyrus entered the city of Babylon without resistance. Consistent with his "return to normalcy" policy, he then issued a decree allowing exiled Jews to return to their homeland.

Pharisees—strict legalists who observed the Law in its smallest detail and elevated the oral traditions to the same level as the written Law. They were believed to have descended from the Hasidim, a group who resisted Hellenism under Seleucid rule.

Philip the Tetrarch (r. 4 BC–AD 34)—son of Herod the Great and Cleopatra of Jerusalem, he ruled areas northeast and east of Galilee and built Caesarea Philippi, named after the Roman emperor Caesar Augustus.

Pilate (r. AD 26–36)—Roman military governor of Judea. At the insistence of the Jews, he ordered Jesus executed by crucifixion.

Pompey—Roman general who captured Jerusalem in 63 BC.

Ptolemy I (r. 323–285 BC)—One of Alexander the Great's four generals; established the Ptolemaic Dynasty in Egypt. After Alexander's death, his empire was divided among his generals rather than his descendants. Ptolemy was the first ruler of Egypt, Daniel 11:5's "King of the south." The name Ptolemy was used to identify subsequent rulers in Egypt.

Ptolemy Philadelphus (r. 285–246 BC)—Egyptian (Ptolemaic) ruler who authorized the translation of the Hebrew Old Testament into Greek (known as the Septuagint).

Publicans—tax collectors or tax farmers under Roman rule. They bought franchises from the Romans to collect taxes and made their money by collecting more than they were required to pay the Romans.

Sadducees—wealthy aristocrats, generally unpopular with the people who controlled the temple. They supported Hellenism and disagreed with the larger party of the Pharisees about interpretation of the Law. They did not believe in resurrection or the existence of angels.

Salome—sister of Herod the Great, who hated his sons by Mariamne (Aristobulus, Alexander); she started a rumor they were plotting to kill Herod. He ordered them strangled.

Samaritans—descendants of the interracial marriages of Jews and Gentiles in Israel (Northern Kingdom). The Assyrians conquered Israel in 722 BC, then relocated Gentiles from other conquered nations into the area. The Jews who married them and adopted some of their religious practices were called Samaritans after Samaria, capital of the Northern Kingdom. Racially pure Jews generally despised Samaritans.

Sanhedrin—the highest religious council in Israel, comprised of seventy members plus the high priest. This high court had the authority to make decisions on matters related to the Law and tradition.

Seleucus I (Nicator)—first ruler of the Syrian (Seleucid) Dynasty (r. 304–281 BC). He had been Ptolemy's general but abandoned him to establish an empire in the north that included Babylonia, Media, and Syria. The Seleucid Empire rivaled the Ptolemaic Empire in Egypt and eventually gained control of Palestine.

Septuagint—Greek version of the Hebrew Old Testament. Jews who lived in Egypt and understood Greek better than Hebrew translated the Old Testament into Greek during the rule of Ptolemy Philadelphus. The standard symbol for the translation is LXX, the Roman numeral for seventy, because according to tradition, seventy Jewish scribes completed the translation in seventy days.

Simon—son of Mattathias, third leader of the Maccabees. After the death of his brother Jonathan, he led the revolt against the Syrians. He declared independence and was installed as high priest for life in 140 BC, an event marking the end of Syrian rule and the beginning of the Hasmonean era.

Synagogue—place of worship for Jews dispersed throughout the ancient Near East and Mediterranean world. The word *synagogue* means "assembly," a gathering of people. The first synagogues, probably established during the Babylonian exile after the temple's destruction, were organized as places of worship, including prayer and the study of the Scriptures.

Tetrarch—a ruler of a fourth of a kingdom. Philip, for example, was tetrarch of an area north and northeast of Galilee.

Tower of Antonia—or Antonia Tower; a citadel (fortress) in Jerusalem Herod the Great built; named after Mark Anthony, connected to the temple's western wall.

Zerubbabel—first leader of the returnees from Babylonian exile. In 538 BC he led about fifty thousand Jews from Babylon to Judea; he also organized the rebuilding of what became known as Zerubbabel's Temple.

Dr. William H. Marty (ThD, Dallas Theological Seminary) is Professor of Bible at Moody Bible Institute and has published two textbooks, *Surveying the New Testament* and *Survey of the Old Testament,* as well as *The Whole Bible Story.* He is unique among Bible college professors in that he teaches and writes on both the New and Old Testaments. Dr. Marty lives with his wife in Chicago. They attend Willow Creek, Chicago, a church they helped start.

Don't Miss
The Whole Bible Story!

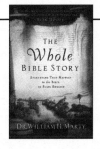

The Bible tells a story. It's a beautiful account of God's love for people throughout history. The events told in the Bible are exciting, tender, and at times awe-inspiring—but often the story can get lost among the laws, genealogies, prophecies, poetry, and instructions. Sometimes we need to get back to what actually happens in the Bible, focusing on the plot and the characters.

In this book, Dr. William Marty retells the entire story of the Bible in one easy-to-read, chronological account. All the stories you remember from childhood—Noah, David, Esther, Daniel, and Jesus—are part of one grand narrative. And that same narrative is the page-turning story of God's love and pursuit of you—one you'll want to read again and again.

The Whole Bible Story by Dr. William H. Marty

Free study guide available at bethanyhouse.com!